ISRAEL
Group Relations in a New Society

ISRAEL

Group Relations in a New Society

ALEX WEINGROD

GREENWOOD PRESS, PUBLISHERS
WESTPORT, CONNECTICUT

Library of Congress Cataloging in Publication Data

Weingrod, Alex.
    Israel : group relations in a new society.

    Reprint of the ed. published for the Institute
of Race Relations by Praeger, New York, in series:
An Institute of Race Relations publication.
    Bibliography: p.
    1. Assimilation (Sociology) 2. Social groups.
3. Israel--Social conditions. I. Title. II. Series: An Institute of Race Relations publication.
[HN761.P32W43 1976]   301.29'5694   76-9027
ISBN 0-8371-8884-9

Originally published in 1965 by Frederick A. Praeger,
Publishers, New York

Reprinted with the permission of Praeger Publishers, Inc.

Reprinted in 1976 by Greenwood Press,
a division of Williamhouse-Regency Inc.

Library of Congress Catalog Card Number 76-9027

ISBN 0-8371-8884-9

Printed in the United States of America

CONTENTS

TABLES

For Bracha

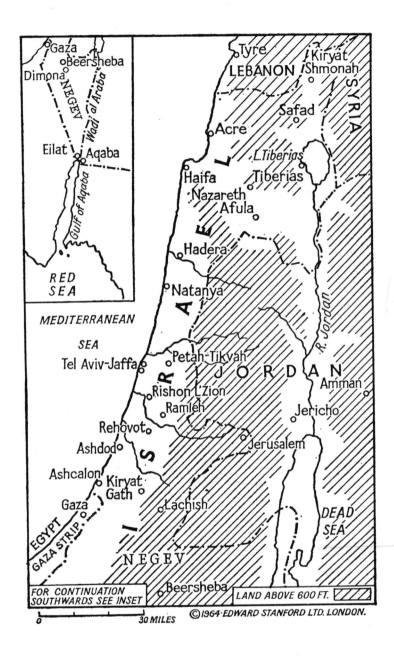

Gaza
Beersheba
Dimona
NEGEV
Wadi' al Araba
Eilat
Aqaba
Gulf of Aqaba
RED
SEA

MEDITERRANEAN

SEA

Tel Aviv-Jaffa

Tyre
LEBANON
Kiryat
Shmonah
SYRIA
Safad
Acre
L.Tiberias
Haifa
Tiberias
Nazareth
Afula
Hadera
Natanya
I   S   R   A   E   L
Petah-Tikvah
JORDAN
Amman
Rishon L'Zion
Ramleh
Jericho
Rehovot
Jerusalem
Ashdod
Ashcalon
Kiryat
Gath
Gaza
Lachish
EGYPT
GAZA STRIP
NEGEV
DEAD
SEA
Beersheba
R. Jordan

FOR CONTINUATION
SOUTHWARDS SEE INSET

LAND ABOVE 600 FT.

0   30 MILES

© 1964·EDWARD STANFORD LTD. LONDON.

I

INTRODUCTION

THIS essay is written as an interpretation of a major—perhaps *the* major—issue in Israeli social life: the problems arising from cultural diversity. Ranging from Yemenite to Russian, from Cochini-Indian to the *sabra** or from Arab to Jew, Israel's population is composed of a great number of culturally defined groups. The question of how these groups relate to one another is the main topic explored in this book.

Some of the issues to be examined were neatly stated in a recent discussion broadcast over the national Israeli radio station. Four youngsters in a regional high school, two of them immigrants, the others native-born *kibbutz* (collective village) youngsters, were interviewed regarding their social relations with one another. How well did these classmates know each other? What the interviewer soon discovered was that the *kibbutz* and the immigrant youngsters had few contacts outside of the classroom. 'We live in different worlds,' a *kibbutz* youngster remarked, 'and we don't try very hard to bring them together.'[1] He went on to explain the separation:

> We [*kibbutz* children] have so many things in common. When we get together we can talk about our own social events, and we just don't have much to talk about with them. For some reason they keep apart from us—and we keep away from them.[2]

This comment may or may not be typical of Israeli schools;

---

* The *Sabras* are the native-born, the second or third-generation Israelis.

other classmates, or different schools, may have different experiences. What is significant, however, is the student's perceptive understanding of some of the reasons for social divisions. To live in different worlds or 'to have so many things in common', provides a basis for sociability; similarities in speech and tradition bind persons to one another, and thereby set them off from others. Just like the *kibbutz* children, immigrants also, abroad in a new and strange world, form inclusive social groups—groups based upon their common origins. Their associations, sympathies and sense of identity are bound together with their fellow immigrants. With its proportionately huge influx of immigrants, Israel has become a multi-ethnic society.

This is a strikingly new development—the pre-1948 Jewish community was much more homogeneous—and it poses new problems for both immigrants and veterans. How do immigrants from, say, Poland and Yemen view one another? How exclusive are the veteran groups? How easily, and by what means, can immigrants become allied to veterans? How do members of the Arab minority and Jewish majority relate to each other? Can a viable state emerge from a society so fragmented?

These are among the main questions considered in this essay. As must be the case in a brief study, however, only selected facts regarding contemporary Israeli society are presented. Indeed, this book concentrates upon Israel's three dominant social cleavages: relationships between immigrants and veterans, between Europeans and Middle Easterners, and between Arabs and Jews. To summarize briefly the book's development: following a short historical sketch (Chapter 1) a series of immigrant responses to Israeli society are examined. These four responses—ambivalence, disaffection, apathy and commitment —are considered to be short-term, alternating states of mind. As general types of response the four categories may equally be valid for the Israeli veteran population, or, for that matter, any population. Unlike veterans, however, immigrants are constantly troubled by their relationship with the national society, and therefore applying these categories to them is especially appropriate. The analysis of these responses (Chapter 3) is followed by a consideration of longer-term trends in immigrant social, economic and political mobility (Chapter 4). The final chapter concludes with an examination of possible forms of a future Israeli society.

Throughout this book immigrants to Israel from countries such as Morocco, Iraq, Yemen, and so forth, are labelled 'Middle Eastern'. This is, it seems to me, a more accurate designation than such oft-used terms as 'Oriental' or 'Afro-Asian': these latter terms are inappropriate, since they tend to lump the immigrants with other populations with whom they have little in common. With the exception of Indian Jews, all of these immigrants come from Islamic countries, and although it is stretched here to include North Africa, the term 'Middle Eastern' is a more appropriate designation.

I am indebted to a number of persons and groups for their assistance in completing this essay. Professors Robert Manners, Benson Saler, Ben Halpern, Max Gluckman and Leonard Fein made many useful suggestions, their comments are gratefully acknowledged, although none of these gentlemen may be held responsible for the material or its interpretation. Brandeis University provided a generous grant for preparing the manuscript, and I should like to thank the University for its support. Mrs. Betty Griffin assisted in carefully editing and typing the manuscript. Finally, I would like to thank the officers of the Institute of Race Relations—and particularly Philip Mason, Naomi Mosbacher, Cleodie Macdonald and Claire Pace—for their extraordinary patience and gentle prodding that enabled the essay to be concluded.

2

CULTURAL FOUNDATIONS

ISRAELI society often seems a mixture of opposites, a jumble of contradictions. Consider these briefly: the land itself is ancient, studded with Biblical memories—but the inhabitants are mainly newcomers, and the shock of immigration lies near to the surface. Beersheba, Lachish, Devorah—these places have the ring of history; but the whitewashed, concrete-block homes that dot the land are nearly all new. Natural resources are practically absent in this tiny country; yet living standards constantly spiral upwards, and there is almost a sense of abundance. The immigrants themselves are incredibly diverse, ranging from sophisticated Central Europeans to feudal Yemenis. There are, so it seems, all manner of Jews, a virtual Babel of colours, customs and tongues. And Arabs too: Bedouin and townsmen, this formerly stolid majority is now a tense minority.

Surely the diversity is great; and yet several organizing elements help to clarify the complexities of Israeli life. First, examining Israel's historic development places contemporary diversity in clearer perspective: examining how and why the groups that make up the society arrived at their present positions is a necessary prelude to understanding present-day life. Second, contemporary social conditions are best understood in relation to the cultural backgrounds of Israel's citizens. Israel is an immigrant-created society, and the immigrants' cultural backgrounds have a decisive influence upon the nation's development. Third, natural factors also influence the nation's social patterns: the size of the state, and the distribution of population, are important factors in national and local life.

4

Understanding these three elements—history, culture, and settlement patterns—places contemporary conditions in proper perspective. It is therefore to these elements that we first turn our attention.

The Formative Period

There is a certain sense in which all of Jewish diaspora history is a prelude to Israel's formation. Jerusalem, or the dream of return to Zion, are recurring themes in Jewish sacred literature. Throughout the centuries there were sporadic small migrations of European and Middle Eastern Jews to the Holy Land. But a truly nationalist migration dates from the birth of modern Zionism. It is therefore to the late nineteenth century—and to Russia in particular—that one must turn for the modern origins of the Jewish State.

Herzl may be the 'father' of political Zionism, but the essential force of Jewish colonization came from Pinsk, not Vienna. As Isaiah Berlin has correctly noted, Russian Jewry stands at the centre of Israel's formation and development.[1] By the last quarter of the nineteenth century Russian Jews were increasingly exposed to secular European civilization. Intellectual and, in its wake, political agitation, began to loosen the grip of traditional Judaism. It was an age of political reform—plot and manœuvre, dedication to ideals, activism—and moving from the ghetto often meant an involvement with radical movements. Those 'intelligentsia' who joined radical groups were only a fraction of the Jewish population; but the repercussions of their acts have been enormous.

Tsarist Russia practised, to use Berlin's phrase, a 'stupid form of despotism'; inept and repressive, it provoked opposition from many segments of the population.[2] But the Jews' lot was especially critical. Anti-semitism was often government policy: veering from mere ostracism to bloody pogroms, it made for continual insecurity in Jewish life. It is hardly surprising that many Russian Jews sought to emigrate: desiring a better life, outraged and fearful of their future, many fled from Russia. Most of these immigrants turned to America, England and other Western countries: New York's Lower East Side, or London's East End, became Jewish ghettos in this period. But

5

others, a comparative handful, chose elsewhere, and migrated to the then Turkish-controlled Palestine. These colonists were the originators of modern Israel.

First generations, 'Mayflower generations', are often critical in a society's development: their traditions form the core of the emerging nation. In the case of Israel, the ideals of the late nineteenth-century Russian immigrants hold vast importance: they shaped, and continue to mould, the institutional basis of Israeli life. However small in number (between 1880 and 1920 only 80,000 Jews immigrated to Palestine) these purposeful, dedicated colonists set their stamp upon the emerging society.

Zionism, socialism and pioneering were the major ideals of this founding generation. Zionism, first of all, called for the creation of a fully autonomous Jewish nation. The immigrants fervently believed that national independence held the only solution to the 'Jewish problem': anti-semitism, the Jews' marginality and rootlessness, would only be solved by the formation of an independent state. Zionism therefore had political, economic and cultural implications—or, to put it differently, the colonists wished to create a total, all-embracing society. In regard to governmental affairs, after the close of World War I, Great Britain was granted mandatory control over Palestine. Shortly thereafter, the Palestinian Jewish community established a series of semi-autonomous political institutions: a national assembly was elected, and the Jewish Agency began to represent the colonists before national and international bodies. A viable economy was the second prerequisite for ultimate independence. The national agencies therefore sponsored economic development activities, as, for example, the purchase of land from Arab owners, or assistance to new agricultural villages.

Cultural autonomy—the third feature of the Zionist programme—is best represented in the renaissance of Hebrew. Previously relegated to sacred occasions, Hebrew became the colonists' language of daily expression, and books and plays were also written in Hebrew. Even though emphasis was placed upon Hebrew, the colonists never severed their ties with modern European culture: they might live in the Middle East, but they were attuned to political and literary movements in the Western world. In addition, the colonists were self-consciously secularist:

6

they rejected orthodox Jewish religious tradition, and sought instead to create a new type of secular culture.

Turning next to socialism, the immigrants' socialist creed was Utopian in outlook. True to their radical past, they wished not merely to establish another nation but hoped, in addition, to invest the nation with their highest ideals—social justice, equality, co-operation, the dignity of labour, and public-oriented development. Society, and man as well, was therefore to be reconstructed. And indeed, the life-style that emerged during this period well expressed their ideals. For example, many immigrants, most of whom came from middle-class, urban backgrounds, became workers. In part this arose from purely practical considerations: there simply were few other jobs available. But physical labour was also imbued with a mystique and considered a virtue: hard work—as stevedores, masons or farmers—was romanticized, and a kind of Tolstoyan 'noble peasant' became the cultural ideal. Allied with this was an emphasis upon personal simplicity: unadorned dress, direct manners, rough foods. This stress upon the 'simple life' became a distinctive feature of the new Jewish society.

If the immigrants' socialism was Utopian, the Histadruth, or General Federation of Jewish Labour, was the concrete vehicle through which socialism was to become realized. Histadruth activities were boundless, and it became, in effect, a 'state-within-a-state'. The new Jewish workers were organized into national unions: militantly fighting for worker rights, the Histadruth early established a progressive code of social legislation. Wage scales were egalitarian in the extreme, so that the incomes of workers, executives and professionals were scarcely differentiated. (The standard story is that, since salaries varied according to the size of the worker's family, a janitor with many children had a larger income than a director of a large Histadruth enterprise with a small family.) In addition to representing worker interests, the Histadruth also became an economic power in its own right: some of the basic 'means of production' (notably transportation and construction) were Histadruth owned or controlled, and numerous local co-operatives were also sponsored by the Histadruth. In effect, this comparative giant gained a major role in the social, economic and political affairs of the nation-to-be: the Histadruth's strength asserted

7

the dominance of a 'welfare-state' form of economy and polity in which public, rather than private industry, held the pre-eminent position.

Pioneering—the third major ideal of the founding generation—expresses the merging of Zionism with socialism. Pioneers were immigrants who, choosing public over private interests, stood ever-ready to undertake national tasks. Road-building, or work in the remote desert, were early pioneer ventures. Pioneering was, however, primarily associated with the new agricultural settlements: the *kibbutz* (collective village), and to a lesser extent the *moshav* (co-operative village), epitomized the pioneer life. These villages were national instruments; each new village claimed additional land for the emerging nation. Moreover, their communal or co-operative form represented a personal expression of Utopian socialism. Idealistic and deeply dedicated, the pioneers formed an élite group—they were the most esteemed members of the colonist society.

This new colonist society was close and intimate. Numerically, it was small, so that many persons could know one another well. More important, the colonists were a homogeneous, highly selected group: the majority were young, and most were also (at least at first) unmarried. Theirs was an almost evangelical enthusiasm: they were passionate in their dedication to national and social ideals. The physical hardships of their lives, and the opposition they faced, also solidified the bonds between them: outbreaks of Arab terror, or opposition to Turkish or British rule, drew them closer together. Then, too, those who could not adjust to the new conditions—and there were many—left Palestine and migrated back to Russia or to the West. All of these factors contributed to the strong communal feelings that epitomized the formative period. But it was mainly the dedication that the immigrants shared in building a new nation that lent the community its keen sense of common purpose.

Communalism did not, however, check the growth of separate political parties: even though the colonists shared a common vision, they differed sharply in regard to the particular forms their society should adopt. As is perhaps characteristic of evangelical movements (and in close parallel to pre-revolutionary Russia) sectarian political parties flourished in the atmosphere of national rebirth. The small community soon

8

included varieties of Marxist and non-Marxist groups, as well as religious, centrist and right-wing parties; and the dominant socialist parties were themselves fragmented between *kibbutz*, *moshav* and urban sectors. Politics were fiercely important: these were not merely competing interest groups, they represented opposed social philosophies. Moreover, since political ideologies were so crucial, the political parties played an expanding role in the new society. The major national institutions, such as the Histadruth and the Jewish Agency, were themselves organized and controlled by the parties. And the parties also engaged in a plethora of social and economic—as well as purely political— activity. The direction of party affairs, and of public matters in general, therefore came to be exercised by national, centralized groups. Even though politics were personalized and highly democratic, national organization and direction became a distinctive feature of the colonization culture.

The period between 1880 and the close of the First World War witnessed a slow, but constant, Jewish immigration. During those forty years large villages (such as Rehovot and Zichron Yaacov) were founded, and the new city of Tel Aviv as well as several score agricultural colonies were also formed. The bulk of the immigrants were East Europeans, and, although numerically a minority, the pioneers among them played leading roles in public affairs. However, even at this formative stage different elements were included within the Jewish population. The Holy Cities of Jerusalem, Safad and Tiberias contained many religious Jews, some of whose families had lived there for hundreds of years. In addition, small bands of Yemenite and Kurdish Jews also migrated to Palestine during the late nineteenth and early twentieth centuries. These immigrants—often followers of a *chacham*, or elder holy-man—tended to settle in tiny clusters; for example, some of the Kurds made their home in Jerusalem, while many Yemenites found work in the orange-groves near Rehovot and Rishon L'Zion. Cultural differentiation was therefore already present during the formative period. But it was small in scale: the European, pioneer element was vibrant and dominant, while the religious and Middle Eastern groups were peripheral. Indeed, these various groups seem to have followed separate paths, with little if any meaningful contact between them.

B

9

This brief sketch of the early phase of Jewish colonization is, certainly, partial and selective: and yet it does stress the spirit and some of the institutions that were then established. Present-day Israeli life continues to be influenced by this initial period. The values and viewpoints of the East European colonists are still powerful forces in modern Israel: pioneering, Utopianism and egalitarianism remain part of the public creed, and they continue to be enunciated by the reigning political élites. Israel has also recently witnessed the growth of a competing middle-class ethic; and, as in so much of the West (and the East), ideologies have become less compelling for new generations. Still, the ideals of the early colonists retain their power: they are part of the dominant culture, and in one way or another they are influential throughout the entire society.

Mass Immigration: Ethnicity Emerges

The Zionist idea conceived of the Jewish State as a haven—a place of refuge to which Diaspora Jews might flee in time of peril. To a limited extent Palestine did become a haven in the period between the two World Wars. For example, thousands of Polish Jews migrated to Palestine during the 1920s and early 1930s. Later, some German Jews who fled Nazi terror also emigrated to Palestine. Population growth during this period was impressive: between 1925 and 1940 the Jewish community grew from 122,000 to 470,000 persons.

More important, this increase was not merely numerical but also encompassed new social elements: unlike the former immigrants, these persons were not self-selected but rather represented a broad spectrum of population. Many of the Poles and Germans did not share the vision of Utopian socialism—they represented a stolid, middle-class ethic, and in the case of German immigrants they also prized their background in 'high culture'. Merchants, shopkeepers or professionals, they maintained a certain detachment and did not fuse with the Russian-led élite. Theirs was a physical separation as well: towns such as Nahariya and Nathanya, as well as sections of Haifa, became heavily populated by middle-class German immigrants.

However, this larger immigration—and the accompanying

cultural heterogeneity—gives only a clue to the much more complex mass-migration that was to follow. The march of events can only be presented here in bare outline form. By the mid-1930s the 'Palestine question' had assumed world prominence: growing in strength, the Jewish community wished for an increased pace of immigration; German anti-semitism produced the 'refugee problem', as thousands of fleeing German-Jews had nowhere to turn; Palestinian Arabs violently opposed any increase in Jewish immigration, and pressed instead for local Arab autonomy; and Britain, the mandatory power, was caught in the anomalous position of pledging support to both the Jewish and the Arab causes, and wishing, as well, to further her own imperial interests. During World War II Jewish immigration virtually ceased. But immediately thereafter, when the pitiful survivors of Hitler's concentration camps appeared, the question of Jewish immigration again became a world issue. However, in the post-World War II climate the issue was not merely immigration, but rather statehood: both Arabs and Jews demanded independence. As passions rose, violence and terror also grew: Jewish extremist groups, such as the Stern Gang and the Irgun, turned to bombing and assassination, as a means of grasping national independence. Caught between conflicting pressures, Great Britain finally tired of a thankless role and placed the entire problem before the United Nations. Events then moved with startling rapidity. The UN decision for the partition of Palestine was taken in November, 1947: autonomous Jewish and Arab states were to be carved-out of the Palestinian territory. Armed hostilities then broke out between Arabs and Jews, and many Arabs fled from the Jewish zones. Finally, in May, 1948, Israel proclaimed its independence and waged a successful war against the invading Arab armies. In this brief, but bloody, succession of events, the long-dreamt-of Jewish State became a reality.

Israel then became a sovereign state—a national government was formed, ministries sprouted, a regular army was organized. But what of the Israeli population: how would independence affect its composition? Mass migration settled this issue, but in a wholly unexpected fashion. The flight of Palestinian Arabs was not anticipated, and yet, almost overnight, hundreds of thousands fled, and Jews became the dominant group in the population. And, at the same time, the rate of Jewish immigration grew enormously. In earlier years immigrants had numbered hundreds, or at most thousands, per year. But now, for the first time, literally tens of thousands clamoured to immigrate. The Jewish population in 1947 numbered approximately 650,000, whereas three years later, following massive migration, it had nearly doubled. It was an unparalleled rate of immigration—although, as the following table shows, it did not last long—and it has completely changed the cultural character of the Jewish community.

TABLE I

Jewish Population of Palestine-Israel, 1882–1962[3]

Year	Population	Year	Population
1882	24,000*	1950	1,203,000
1900	50,000*	1952	1,450,000
1914	85,000*	1954	1,526,000
1925	122,000*	1956	1,667,500
1935	355,200*	1958	1,810,100
1945	563,800*	1960	1,911,200
1948	649,600*	1962	2,068,900

* =approximation

How did mass immigration alter the Jewish community? First, it produced a socially mixed population: while the pre-1948 population was largely self-selected, post-1948 immigration was primarily an evacuation of total populations. During 1948 and 1949 the European Jewish refugee camps were closed, and more than 70,000 concentration camp survivors emigrated *en masse* to Israel. Beginning in 1949, and continuing through 1951, 220,000 Polish and Rumanian Jews also emigrated. In this same period 40,000 Yemenites—nearly the entire Yemenite Jewish community—were transferred to Israel. And concurrently 125,000 Iraqi Jews were airlifted to new homes in Israel. Large-scale immigration also began from North African countries such as Libya, Tunisia and Morocco. Later, in the period between 1953 and 1960, more selective immigration measures were introduced, and the pace of immigration fell. Yet even with this decline the Jewish community was irrevocably altered. Mass immigration brought an entire spectrum of persons: the sick and the healthy, the rich and poor (they were mainly poor), those with large families as well as those who were unmarried, the dull and the well-educated. It created, at once, an enormous heterogeneity in a society that had formerly been so selective and homogeneous.

Moreover, the post-1948 immigrants were not grounded in ideology. Zionism and Utopian socialism drew many of the pre-state immigrants to Palestine. But the European or Middle Eastern evacuees were more 'pushed' than 'pulled': although messianism was an important element in their migration, in most cases the immigrants fled from their native countries because of insecurity caused by political and economic upheavals. The Russian colonists' ideals of socialism, co-operation or equality had little meaning for these immigrants: indeed, they were often incomprehensible to them. Mass immigration therefore introduced a new *majority* population which had little understanding of, or sympathy with, the ideals of the colonization culture.

Finally, mass immigration also introduced large groups drawn from a completely different civilization: Middle Eastern Jews. This was another unanticipated development: although small numbers of Yemenite, Kurdish and Moroccan Jews had earlier migrated to Palestine, the massive immigration that commenced in 1948 was never foreseen. Table II records this sudden rise of Middle Easterners in the Jewish population: in 1948 Middle Easterners accounted for 8·8 per cent of the Jewish population, while in 1962 the percentage had more than tripled. What is more, together with their Israeli-born children Middle Easterners now include roughly 42 per cent of the total Jewish population—and since their birth-rate is substantially higher than Europeans they are likely, in the near future, to become the majority group.[4]

The experience, customs and even appearance of Middle Eastern Jews differ fundamentally from their European brethren. Long resident in Muslim lands, their life-style closely resembled their Muslim neighbours. For many of them—the Yemenites and Kurds, for example—Israel represented their first contact with modern Western civilization. For others— Tunisians, some Moroccans, Iraqis—partial contact had previously been established, and these immigrants were already in the throes of a cultural transition. Yet for all of these new-comers Israel represented a social revolution: it introduced them to a different technology, new kinds of social and political relations, and a novel system of social values. This plunge into a new type of society highlighted the differences between Middle Easterners and Europeans: they were observably different groups. Mass immigration therefore magnified the extent of cultural separation within the Jewish community. In effect, it produced a new type of society, a society composed of large, culturally-differentiated groups. This splitting of society along cultural lines has surely been the most significant social development in Israel's brief history.

TABLE II

Jewish Population, 1948–1962
By Continent of Birth[5]

	European	Middle East	Israeli
1948	54·8	8·8	35·4
1952	45·3	27·6	27·1
1956	37·7	29·4	32·9
1960	35·1	27·8	37·1
1962	33·5	28·0	38·5

Arabs and Jews

Thus far little has been said regarding the Arab population. But certainly this group, too, must be considered in an analysis of inter-group relations in Israeli society. Arabs had been the majority in Palestine. Mainly composed of village-dwelling peasants, but also including nomadic Bedouin and townsmen, the Arab populace violently opposed Jewish colonization. Terrorism and Arab-Jewish clashes were frequent: the political aspirations of the two groups were wholly at odds. As a consequence, the pre-1948 Arab and Jewish societies were almost entirely separate from one another: each group developed its own social, economic and political institutions, and these inter-twined only occasionally. Then, with the 1948 partition of Palestine into Jewish and Arab states, the new political order led to a total shift in Arab-Jewish relations.

The question of why the sudden, desperate flight of Palestinian Arabs to the surrounding countries took place has been the subject of continuous, impassioned controversy. The issue is complex, and it cannot be adequately treated here. But—in brief—it is probably fair to conclude that this wholesale population transfer resulted from two factors: panic and miscalculation on the part of the Arabs themselves; and the policies of the Israeli authorities. Local struggles between Jews and Arabs spread panic among Arab villagers and townsmen. Moreover, the Arab leadership advised their followers to leave, however temporarily, while the invading armies of Egypt, Jordan, Iraq, Syria and Lebanon moved to crush the Israelis. The flight was contagious—between January and March, 1948, hundreds of thousands of local Arabs fled to Egypt and Jordan. Once this movement had begun, the Israeli authorities did little to stop it: although unanticipated, this flight was perceived as a quick way to 'solve the Arab question'. Thus, in a period of months, the previously Arab majority became a minority: according to estimate there were in 1947 some 740,000 Arabs in the territory that became Israel;[6] by 1949, only 160,000 remained. The Arab community has since grown in size—its rate of natural increase is prodigious, and it now includes nearly a quarter of a million persons—but it remains a small, cloistered minority.[7]

Who Lives Where?

This discussion has thus far been focused upon immigrants. To complete this background sketch, it will also be useful to describe the country's main physical features, and to indicate how these are linked with social developments.

The first point to note is that the country itself is small; in fact, it is tiny. Israel is a thin sliver of a country: in length it measures a full 426 miles, but for much of this distance it is phenomenally narrow. Just north of Tel Aviv the distance between the sea and the Jordan border is a mere twelve miles! The width increases in the southern Negev region to a maximum of seventy miles, but at no point is there the breadth that characterizes other Middle Eastern countries. Borders are everywhere present: in each direction (save westward, towards the Mediterranean) one almost immediately meets borders that cannot be crossed, and that are dangerous. Major segments of the country are nearly islands surrounded by foreign land. The best example of physical isolation is the city of Jerusalem: cut in half between the new Jewish city and the Jordanian-held Old City, Jerusalem is tenuously attached to the tiny body that is the rest of the country.

Small size is a major factor in Israeli social life. No section of the country is truly remote from others, and the country as a whole has an immediate, physical unity. There are, to be sure, striking differences between the various sections: Israel's physiognomy is richly varied, ranging from the cool Jerusalem hills to the deep depression near the Dead Sea, and from the densely packed coastal strip to the harsh Negev desert. But these differences do not lead to regional fragmentation. There is, for example, no true 'Israeli regionalism': there is nothing in Israel to compare with the American 'North' and 'South', or with a British 'Wales'. The area is too limited, the population too small, for such differentiation to take place. The different segments are closely knit into a single national unity.

Smallness in scale is also emphasized by the presence of a modern road and rail system. The road-grid is extensive, and the railroads, although not fully developed, also reach out to the major population centres. No point in the entire country is more than a six or seven hours' journey from Tel Aviv. This, too, lends a sense of unity to the land.

Coupled with the small population, small physical size has a pervasive influence upon Israeli society. For one thing, it leads to the kind of society amenable to central direction. This is not to say that the tendencies in Israeli life towards political and economic centralization are merely derived from small size: other factors are surely more important. And yet, given a compact physical setting the chances for centralization are increased. In addition, the small scale of the society also promotes a sense of immediacy and personalism. Personalities and events in one section are well known in other sections. Social networks are often national in scope—contacts between persons and groups easily cross the entire country. It is for this reason that innovations and cultural fashions are communicated so quickly throughout the entire society; indeed, changes redound swiftly across the entire social structure.

A second point to be made regarding physical setting is that, in regard to natural resources, Israel is a comparatively poor country: there are few easily exploitable natural resources, and the continuing conflict with the neighbouring Arab states has cut the country off from her natural trading partners. Two-thirds of the countryside is classed as cultivable, but the agricultural potential is limited. The first four or five years following the establishment of the state were lean years, and food shortages were frequent; since then, however, agricultural growth has been impressive, and Israel now produces abundant quantities of fruit, poultry, vegetables and dairy products. (Wheat and beef are still mainly imported from abroad.) Industrial development has also proceeded rapidly: beginning from a small base, a variety of small and medium-sized factories have been built during the past sixteen years. However, these factories, whether automotive assembly plants or diamond polishing shops, depend wholly or partially upon imported raw materials: fuel, timber, iron and a host of other basic raw materials must all be imported. Israel's exports, on the other hand, are limited: citrus from the groves along the coastal strip, or minerals from the Dead Sea region, are exported in sizeable quantity, but the trade balance continues to show a growing gap between imports and exports. For example, in 1962 Israeli exports amounted to $486,000,000, while imports numbered $887,000,000.[8] As is well-known, this uneven trade-balance is adjusted through vast foreign loans and other financial support: reparation funds from Germany, loans from the United States and other Western sources, as well as monies contributed by overseas Jewish communities, yearly inject large sums into the economy. Without these funds, Israel's standard of living would certainly plummet drastically. These facts explain the paradox of the Israeli economy: a naturally poor nation, and yet a continually upward-spiralling standard of living. (Between 1953 and 1958 real wages climbed at the rate of 4·7 per cent per year —a phenomenal increase—so that by 1958 Israeli per capita income compared favourably with European nations such as Austria, Finland and Holland.)[9]

These economic 'facts of life' bear directly upon social and political relations. The funds flowing into the country have, by and large, been placed at the disposal of government groups, rather than private corporations or individuals. The government, the Jewish Agency and the Histadruth—the 'trinity' of Israeli public institutions—are the main recipients of public funds, and they have, in turn, channelled this capital into immigrant absorption, economic development and defence activities. Many thousands of homes for immigrants, an expanded school system, literally hundreds of new villages, huge pipelines, modern armaments—these are among the multitude of projects undertaken by government groups. It is no exaggeration to say that the entire country has been transformed by these activities.

At the same time, however, this emphasis upon public economic activity results in an economy that is tightly centralized and controlled: government administrative regulations (over costs and prices) are extensive, and government-sponsored enterprises in housing, agriculture and industry have a determining influence upon the economy as a whole. Even though there have been recent tendencies towards liberalization, the public sector dominates the private: the economy is government-planned and, to a considerable extent, government-administered.

This proliferation of public economic activities is also reflected in the Israeli occupational distribution: almost 30 per cent of Israeli wage-earners are employed in service occupations, and more than 20 per cent work in government groups. As

TABLE III

Labour Force Distribution
Israel and Other Countries (by per cent)[10]

	Israel (*1958*)	Austria (*1951*)	Italy (*1951*)	Switzerland (*1950*)
Agriculture	17·6	32·2	40·0	16·5
Manufacturing	21·7	28·3	22·8	38·5
Construction	9·8	8·0	7·1	8·1
Commerce and Banking	12·3	8·8	12·4	11·6
Transport and Communication	6·8	5·3	3·8	4·6
Services	29·8	15·3	8·1	19·8
Other	2·0	2·0	5·8	0·9

Table III shows, this distribution ranks high in comparison with a selected group of European nations, and the proportions employed in industry and agriculture are correspondingly low. Public agencies are the major employers: on the one hand, they are engaged in production (shipping or mining) and service (health and education) activities, and, at the same time, the ministerial bureaucracies are also very extensive. The early Russian colonists had hoped to 'invert the pyramid' of traditional Jewish occupations—to increase the number of workers, and decrease the number of merchants and clerks—and yet the proportion of clerks and professionals remains high.

Thus far we have glanced at Israel's natural contours and economic structure. It is, in addition, necessary to examine how the various social groups are distributed within the country.

The first point to note is that the population as a whole is unevenly distributed: the comparatively huge Negev desert zone, which includes 70 per cent of the total land area, contains only 9 per cent of the Jewish population, whereas the Tel Aviv zone, which includes less than 1 per cent of the land area, includes 35 per cent. Tel Aviv forms the centre of a sprawling urban cluster, ranging from Rehovot in the south to Nathanya in the north, and this densely packed zone has become the nation's cultural, financial and administrative core. The three major cities—Tel Aviv, Haifa and Jerusalem—together compose 55 per cent of the total Jewish population; and more than 80 per cent of the Jewish population live in cities or towns. In brief, Israel is highly urbanized, and population concentration is dense in the centre of the country, but becomes uneven and fragmented as one moves to the southern and northern peripheries.

Not only is the population as a whole unevenly distributed, the major ethnic and religious groups also tend to cluster in different zones. Spatial separation is particularly striking in regard to the Arab minority. Nearly 80 per cent of Israeli Arabs reside in the northern section of the country, while another 15 per cent (the 28,000 Israeli Bedouin) are concentrated in the area south of Beersheba. Arabs are not a majority group in either region, but they do compose a large minority. Moreover,

Arab villages or towns are separate from Jewish communities: for example, Nazareth now includes both the old, traditional centre—populated entirely by Arabs—and a new adjoining town composed of Jewish immigrants. This pattern is repeated throughout the countryside. It is also important to note that 80 per cent of Israeli Arabs live in rural communities, and 20 per cent in urban areas, while among Jews the proportions are exactly the reverse. These statistics indicate the gross differences between the two groups: Jews and Arabs are spatially separated, and the kind of community each typically lives in is also different.

Population clusters are also significant among Jews. Zones of settlement follow three main lines: secular and religious enclaves, ethnic neighbourhoods, and also veteran, and immigrant sectors. Beginning with the latter, the veteran pre-1948 groups are mainly concentrated in the three major cities, while post-state immigrants are located in new towns in the north and south, or in housing estates on the fringes of the major cities. For example, towns like Beersheba, Dimona and Elath in the south, or Kiryat Shmonah and Nazareth in the north, are primarily composed of recent immigrants, with veterans a distinct minority. Within the major cities, veterans predominate in the inner core, while immigrants are concentrated on the fringes; thus Jerusalem's élite Rechavia district, or the fashionable northern section of Tel Aviv, consists mainly of veterans, while housing estates in Katamon or Jaffa are limited to new immigrants. There is, to be sure, some 'mixing' in the cities—socially mobile immigrants move into the inner, veteran areas—but, in general, immigrants and newcomers are residentially separate.

There are, in addition, distinctions between the immigrant groups themselves. Despite government attempts to 'mix' the immigrants—this will later be described at greater length—in most cases each immigrant group forms a relatively distinct cluster: immigrants who share a common language and tradition have tended to join together, and thereby formed ethnic neighbourhoods or nearly entire communities. Most of the 280 immigrant farming villages (*moshav olim*) consist mainly of immigrants from a single country, and the cities and towns also contain zones populated mainly by Yemenites, Moroccan or other immigrants. Tel Aviv has a 'Yemenite section', Jerusalem a 'Kurdish quarter', Ashcalon a 'Polish neighbourhood', and so forth.

The distinction between religious and secular groups is also significant in several communities. Religious enclaves in Jerusalem and Tel Aviv, for example, include groups who maintain an intensely orthodox way of life. In these neighbourhoods travel is forbidden on the Sabbath, and the modes of dress and speech follow centuries-old traditions.

How Many Israels?

Residential separation between groups immediately suggests additional questions. How much social interaction is there between persons living in different zones—between Algerians and Rumanians, for example? What positions do immigrants and veterans hold *vis-à-vis* one another? Do the immigrants retain their cultural differences—or are immigrants and veterans drawing closer together? Or (to put it differently), how many Israels are there? What is the significance of the social cleavages and social bonds that criss-cross Israeli society?

These questions are the main topics explored in this essay: having examined some aspects of Israel's historical development, we turn next to an analysis of group relations. But what groups should be considered, and which relations should be examined? For surely there are many Israels: there exists in Israel—as in all modern societies—a great range of diversity: Israeli-born and immigrant, immigrants of ten years' standing and those who landed a month ago, the Russian-born élite and the 'outsiders', Yemenites and Poles, religious and free-thinker, Jew and Arab, *kibbutz* member and city merchant, wealthy and poverty-stricken. Each of these (and there are many more) is a distinct cultural world: there are shared elements of tradition within each of these groups that mark them off from others. It will not be possible to consider each of these groups: that analysis would require a much more elaborate presentation. But it will be possible to examine relations between several key groups: specifically, between veterans and immigrants, Europeans and Middle Easterners, and Jews and Arabs. These groups have been selected since they are the major blocs within Israeli society—they are the main elements in the social mosaic —so that relations between them are likely to determine the society's future shape.

3

IMMIGRANT RESPONSES

THE main purpose of the last chapter was to explore the dominant structural and cultural features of Israeli society. In this chapter the focus shifts to the ways immigrants respond to their new setting. What conditions define the 'immigrant experience' for a newly-arrived family from Poland, Tunisia or Iraq, and how have immigrants reacted to these new conditions?

Surely it is difficult to generalize regarding 'the immigrant experience': there are many different kinds of immigrants—the old, the physically strong, the former Zionist, the aged Moroccan rabbi, the Hungarian doctor; and there are also many different social contexts—some immigrants have homes in cosmopolitan cities, others live in tiny villages, some live near their relatives, others are wholly isolated. Moreover, an immigrant has various 'experiences', he performs many roles, in such varied contexts as his daily work, recreational activities, political groups, religious occasions, and so forth. A typology of immigrant responses would have to show how these factors and situations (as well as others) influence an immigrant's reaction to his new social context. Unfortunately, there is little precise comparative information showing how individuals and groups have responded to different social situations: little systematic research of this kind has been carried out. Nevertheless, some of the material collected in studies of immigrants can provide a beginning basis for generalization. It is possible to conceive a number of typical responses to Israeli life.

Ambivalence, apathy, disaffection and commitment designate a range of immigrant responses. These categories are related to the question: how do immigrants 'feel about' their new life, and how do they relate to their new society? It is important to recognize that the categories do not so much refer to actual people, as to their changing states of mind or varying modes of participation in society. The categories themselves are 'closed', but individual immigrants shift from one to the other. Indeed, to some extent each immigrant, at one time or another, is likely to express all of these responses. What determines the response is the particular social content, and, as contexts change, or the immigrant's insight changes, so too does the response differ. Of course, for some persons the response is more permanent—no matter what the context may be, some continue to be 'apathetic'—but for most immigrants 'apathy' or 'disaffection' is a temporary, fluctuating condition.

These categories are abstract and general, and they need more precise definition. Let us briefly consider their meaning.

Ambivalence* refers to a state of conflicting emotions, and to the strains and indecision that result from internal conflict. It is an expression of endless uncertainty—a kind of 'love-hate' relationship. For example, an immigrant may delight in his new-found status as a member of a predominantly Jewish society, but, at the same time, be frustrated by the sense of belonging to the 'out-group'. Or, to use a different illustration, an immigrant may agree that he has bettered himself materially, yet still complain that others have advanced at a more rapid rate, and, moreover, advanced at his expense. Ambivalence is the product of contrary tugs of emotion such as these.

Ambivalence represents something of a middle course, an uncertain, restrained response to the new Israeli environment. Apathy differs from ambivalence in that the apathetic do not feel tugs of emotion, but rather lack emotional or social involvement. Apathetic immigrants are those who, as it were, stand apart on the side, seemingly uninvolved with their new situation.

---

* Waller Zenner has used the term 'ambivalence' to describe Middle Eastern (specifically Syrian) Jews' mixed responses to 'traditional' and 'modern' culture. While this meaning is subsumed in the definition presented here, ambivalence refers not only to conflicts between the 'old' and the 'new', but also to the mixed responses immigrants express to their new Israeli situation.[1]

They have no deep emotional commitments: they are neither frustrated nor cheered, but rather, withdrawn in despair or confusion, they passively accept their lot. This, too, may be considered to be a restrained response. Disaffection and commitment, on the other hand, are active, definite reactions. Disaffection refers to a condition of being cut off from the norms and customs of one's society: to be disaffected is to reject the conventions of everyday living. These immigrants are not merely mildly unhappy; they bitterly dislike the positions they hold. Conversely, those who are committed embrace their society's major patterns of behaviour, and affirm its values and viewpoints. The committed believe in their society, and they are involved in it. Unlike the disaffected, they discover personal meaning and satisfaction in society's institutions.

Immigrant responses can be sorted into these four alternating moods. But if these are typical responses, what are they responsive to? What are the social conditions that immigrants face?

Pioneer, Suburbanite and 'Sabra'

The pre-state society—that small society dominated by European colonists—this is the society that immigrants must respond to: their traditions must, somehow, either be made to converge with, or remain separate from, the traditions of the old-time settlers. However, just as immigrant responses are varied, so too there are strikingly different, even contradictory, customs and expectations expressed by members of the veteran society. There is no unanimity among veterans—there are, rather, different conceptions of the desirable. Broadly speaking (and simplifying greatly) three cultural modes compete within the veteran society: the old, heroic pioneer ethic; a newer, increasingly influential middle class style of life; and an as yet imprecise, but none the less potent, native-born, or *sabra*, tradition. Each of these three acts as a model for immigrants— each presents them with different expectations and interests— and immigrants are therefore influenced by, and may choose between, these different, competing cultural modes.

Public service, the positive value of co-operation, personal modesty and simplicity, egalitarianism, the dignity of labour— these are some of the main emphases of the pioneer ethic.

c   25

Within the veteran society these values are exemplified by the *kibbutzim* and *moshavim*, the communal and co-operative villages. Comparatively few immigrants are, however, exposed to these socially-radical communities: very few join *kibbutzim*, although larger numbers have become employees in *kibbutz* or *moshav* enterprises.* However (and of much greater consequence), these values are also enunciated by the major national institutions: the government, the Jewish Agency and Histadruth. Indeed, Utopian socialist ideals compose the 'public ideology'; government and government-linked groups promote and disseminate the pioneer ethic throughout the land. For example, the school system and the army consciously seek to inculcate pioneering virtues among immigrant youth, and government policy has favoured settling immigrants in co-operative agricultural settlements. These were the orientations of the veteran élites during the formative period, and since that group still retains political control it continues to be the public ideology. The pioneer ethic therefore retains official prominence; in many respects it is to this ethic that immigrants have had to respond.

The political leadership exhorts the populace to remain true to the pioneer goals; and yet, at the same time, more materialist, less public-spirited traditions have become increasingly potent. 'Pioneering' may be the public ideology, but it is not necessarily the guide for personal behaviour. The veteran community has, since 1948, been undergoing a 'crisis in pioneering': goals of national service have been downgraded, and formal state institutions have replaced voluntary groups. To some extent these tendencies were always present in the colonization community, but the colonists' extreme dedication to the

---

* Not only have few immigrants joined *kibbutzim*, these communities have themselves grown increasingly conservative during the past decade. The fact that *kibbutzim* hire immigrant workers (a practice contrary to the orthodox view of the *kibbutz* as a classless society) is indicative of a growing conservative trend. *Kibbutz* living standards are also comparatively high—housing is often excellent, schools are on a par with city-schools, members receive larger personal allotments—so that the 'kibbutz model' often appears to verge upon that of the middle class. At the same time, however, *kibbutz* practice and ideology does continue to stress the older, heroic values.

ideals of state building muted the expression of purely personal interests. The new creed emphasizes middle-class values; private, rather than public, goals have become vital for many persons. 'Middle class' is not restricted to merchants or lawyers; on the contrary, it also includes high-level government administrators, army officers or skilled technicians. The pursuit of private interest now animates broad segments of Israeli society: immigrants may become attracted to a quite different model in the veteran community, exemplified by urban 'café society', the newly fashionable suburbs or vacations in Spain. Side by side with the heroic, spartan pioneer there stands the consumption-oriented, middle-class suburbanite.

The *sabra* tradition—the third model—is less easily characterized. The term *sabra* refers to the desert cactus: hard and prickly on the outside, but substantial and sweet underneath. The native-born (or so it is felt) have these qualities: they bristle outwardly, but beneath that cool exterior there is an inner warmth. How do *sabras* differ from pioneers or the new middle classes? Some *sabras* are pioneers, and others are members of the middle class: but even when they fill these roles they are different from the older generation. As pioneers they are less heroic, more pragmatic, and as suburbanites they are uncertain of their new-found affluence, and wonder whether they have really discovered the 'good life'. The army is probably the best example of a *sabra* institution: indeed, it is a *sabra* preserve, in which only the native-born have reached high ranks. The army is methodical, cool, often brilliant; officers are action-oriented, and suspicious of ideology. Emphasis is placed upon bravery, but also upon modesty. *Sabras* in the army serve the nation—but in a different way, and with a different style, from their forbears.

The immigrants, newcomers in a strange land, must learn to cope with these different cultural models. However, even though the models differ, they also share certain characteristics: several of their underlying assumptions are similar.

First, these veteran models are all European, or Western, in orientation. From architecture to women's fashions, or from *kibbutz* reading-room to Friday night town parties, each of the three models is emphatically Western. (Although there are many second- and third-generation Middle Easterners, the *sabra* stereotype is decidedly European. Indeed, third-generation

27

Yemenites or Iraqis are often labelled *yeleidei ha'aretz* or 'children born in the country', in order to distinguish them from *sabras*; the latter term is reserved for Europeans, or for those Middle Easterners who have successfully adopted European modes of conduct.) Tel Aviv and Jerusalem have more in common with Paris and Warsaw than with Amman or even Cairo: the translations of current English or continental plays into Hebrew, the frantic pace of commercial life, or the modelling of expectations after middle-high fashions—all these attest to the Western cast of this dominant segment. In short, pioneers, suburbanites or *sabras* are wholly committed to Western ideals, and in fact form part of an ever-expanding Euro-American civilization.

Second, each of these groups is reformist in outlook: reformism, a kind of missionary zeal, is another common characteristic. Neither pioneers nor businessmen have been tolerant of cultural differences; on the contrary, they have insisted upon conformity with their own traditions. The potential converts, the objects of reform, are the post-state immigrants: *mizug ha'galuyot*, the 'mixing' of immigrant groups, was early proclaimed as state policy, and deliberate efforts have been made to 'absorb' the immigrants. The motives underlying this cultural crusade are readily apparent: immigrants outnumber the European veterans, and they therefore appear to threaten the cultural foundations so carefully hewn during the formative period. In fact, however, the intent has not been merely to 'mix' the immigrants (which, after all, implies some preservation of cultural elements) but rather to transform them. 'We want to turn them into Israelis'—this is the oft-repeated, classic statement of the reformers' aims. The immigrants—Yemenite peddlers, Iraqi merchants, Polish tradesmen—are all, it is hoped, to be reborn as 'Israelis'. The exact model is, however, unclear. Who is 'the Israeli'? The open-shirted pioneer—the acquisitive middle classes—the *sabra*? The public ideology dramatizes the pioneer: yet surely other models are followed by many immigrants. Nevertheless, while the models conflict with one another, each emphasizes change: the press and the radio, the national institutions and the educational system, even the grocer on the street—all join together in the movement to restructure and reform the immigrants' behaviour.

Change in a Western direction is therefore a pervading force in the immigrants' situation: no matter which model they follow, they must learn to cope with these features of the veteran society. What changes, then, have taken place? What attitudes predominate in veteran-immigrant relations? And how do these relations influence the immigrants' response— what causes ambivalence, apathy, disaffection or commitment?

To understand these responses more fully the immigrant experience needs to be explored in greater depth. Three dimensions of immigrant life are particularly sensitive for clarifying these responses: immigrant occupations, immigrant community and family ties, and veteran-immigrant social relations. These dimensions hardly exhaust the complexities of the newcomers' role in Israeli society; but, in so far as they encompass some crucial features of the immigrant experience, studying these topics does reveal the bases for the immigrants' response.

The World of Work and Things

Immigrants the world over must normally adopt new occupations: immigrants to the United States or Australia, for example, have had to adjust to new kinds of jobs. Those who move from farms to cities experience similar changes. In the case of Israel, however, the occupational transition was particularly acute: the immigrants poured into the country at an unprecedented rate, and the limited fund of natural resources was strained in order to provide them with the barest essentials. Moreover, their previous occupations were not at all adaptive to Israeli conditions. On the contrary: there was an almost total discrepancy between the skills the immigrants brought with them and the country's needs. During the decade between 1950 and 1960, 37 per cent of immigrant males were former artisans or industrial workers (the industrial workers were from small enterprises), 17 per cent were small merchants and peddlers, 13 per cent had administrative or clerical backgrounds, and the remaining 19 per cent were scattered in other occupations.[2] As is apparent, most immigrants were concentrated in such 'traditional' Jewish occupations as commerce, crafts and the professions. Israel's needs, however, were not for petty merchants and tailors, but rather for modern industrial and construction workers, technicians, farmers or skilled mechanics. The immigrants were therefore directed to new occupations: the traditional skills were replaced by new ones. For some, this meant intensive job-retraining, at which specialized trades were taught. But for most immigrants the alternatives narrowed themselves to various kinds of unskilled or semi-skilled labour: public works of various kinds, farming, and a variety of other physically demanding jobs. For example, in 1960 24 per cent of the immigrants from Middle Eastern countries were employed in farming, and another 14 per cent worked in construction and public works projects: these were all new, demanding occupations, and they suggest a good deal regarding an immigrant's transition.[3]

Becoming a farmer, a construction worker or a labourer in a public-works project was a harsh, often gruelling, change. Imagine the shopkeeper from Baghdad turned stone-mason, the Moroccan peddler become farmer, or the Rumanian merchant planting trees in a government afforestation project. These were not voluntary shifts—they were not willing pioneers serving the nation—but were rather entered into since there were no other alternatives. Changes in occupation were particularly difficult for the older immigrants: how could a man become a manual labourer in his adult years; how could he find satisfaction in these dull, menial tasks? In addition to the physical difficulties, the new jobs usually represented a downward plunge in social status. The former merchant who farmed lost esteem in his own eyes, as well as in the eyes of his fellow immigrants. Even more than physical discomfort, this decline in personal status was a bitter shock to many.

Not only did mass immigration lead to gross shifts in occupation, it also drew many persons who were unable to enter the work force: the old or widowed, the disabled, the blind or chronically ill. Large numbers of these 'social cases', and their families, were included in the mass evacuations. In one form or another they have become dependents of the state: some were hospitalized, others drew pensions, and still others were provided with a monthly income by employment in public works projects. A recent estimate suggests that, in 1962, nearly 300,000 persons—an eighth of the total population—fell into the category of publicly supported persons and their families.[4]

Not all of these persons are immigrants, but the vast majority certainly are. Thus, in addition to those who experienced difficulty in finding new occupations, health and age factors caused many to be unable to adjust.

This bleak picture no doubt extends to a sizeable proportion of immigrants. Yet not all of the newcomers were forced into new occupations: some, such as professionals, small shopkeepers and artisans, did continue in their previous work. Nor is it likely that changes in occupation were always unrewarding and harsh: some immigrants found new occupational niches that were for them vital and stimulating.

What is more, even when the change was difficult the striking fact is that many immigrants have made successful occupational adjustments. The immigrants were unprepared and unskilled—but either because of or in spite of this gap, many have learned to perform their new work roles. The experience in farming is particularly instructive. Since 1949 more than 125,000 immigrants were directed to new agricultural villages, where they were required to adopt a farming career. Many later left their villages; in some instances entire communities collapsed, as apathy or factional disputes set in among the settlers; but the majority remained, and many immigrants have since become successful, in some cases even affluent, farmers. The striking fact is that recent immigrants from Yemen, Tunisia or Poland, hardly any of whom had ever before farmed, have become relatively expert in the use of modern machinery, engage in complex speculative transactions and direct their own communities. The recent abundance in agricultural produce is largely a result of the success of these new villages. Equally successful adaptations have also been made in other occupations, most notably in industry and construction. The immigrant labour force has become increasingly skilled, and now performs with relative efficiency. In summary, many immigrants have shown skill in adopting the new technology: there have been no evident blocks to taking on Western techniques or forms of organization.

This last point—the adoption by immigrants of a Western technology—is a critical one. Whether their model be the pioneer or the fashionable middle class, immigrants as a group have rapidly adopted certain Western modes of behaviour.

Among European immigrants this transition has of course been simpler. Yet it has also encompassed the Middle Easterners. The Yemenite immigrants who, one is told, had at first to be initiated into all kinds of Western gadgetry ('They didn't know what a shower was—they'd never seen a toothbrush') now use the 'very latest' items with perfect aplomb. Middle Easterners, and certainly Europeans, work on assembly lines, make purchases on the instalment plan and flock to the movies. Moreover, whether or not an immigrant has adjusted to his new work role, immigrants as a group have adopted the personal consumption habits and aspirations of the veteran Europeans. Immigrants want what the veterans (whether middle class or pioneer) want, or already have: a radio, stove, refrigerator, motor scooter or larger apartment. So far as consumption items are concerned, there is unanimity of desire. And, in fact, increasing numbers of immigrants achieve these consumption goals: each year more families own radios, washing machines and refrigerators. Of course, this has been an uneven rise; as will be made clear in the next chapter, the income of some segments of the population has risen more quickly than that of others. Yet the major fact is that all of the immigrant groups—just as the veterans— partake in an expanding consumption horizon, and all increasingly share some of the same consumption habits.

Community and Family

A second dimension of the immigrant experience is to be found in the new ties forged between the immigrants themselves. The shock of a new land has tended to draw immigrants closer to one another: faced with a new language, as well as unfamiliar work and residence conditions, persons stemming from the same country were often drawn together. In part, these associations were the result of the pace of mass-immigration: as immigrants from, say, Poland or Iraq, flowed into the country, they were dispatched *en masse* to towns and villages where housing was available, and they therefore often lived in contiguous neighbourhoods. In addition, informal 'chains of migration' also pulled the immigrants together; cousins or old comrades sought one another out, and social links between them were re-established. These facts explain how neighbourhoods or even entire communities became ethnic-group concentrations.

Within the neighbourhood itself, associations between immigrants might centre around the local synagogue, or they might find expression in visiting and mutual assistance. Of course, new friendships also developed between persons from different countries: at work, or in one's housing estate, spontaneous meetings sometimes grew into lasting associations. Yet, in general, an immigrant's primary bonds were to people 'like themselves': for example, when questioned regarding their social relations with neighbouring villagers, Iraqi settlers responded that they rarely saw the Moroccans, Tunisians and Hungarians who lived *near* to them, but that they sometimes visited other Iraqi settlers who lived miles away!

These informal ethnic-group ties were, of course, contrary to the official expectations for *mizug ha'galuyot*—for group mixing. Government officials wished to diminish intra-group ties: for this reason entire villages, housing estates or even sections of larger communities were often consciously designed to include Poles, Yemenites, North Africans, Hungarians, and so forth. These 'mixed' immigrants would, it was hoped, fashion wider social contacts, and adopt new forms of behaviour. These hopes were not often realized, however: alone, and feeling isolated, members of each group associated with their fellows. They might not necessarily be old friends, but, at the very least, they spoke the same language.

In addition to informal groups, immigrants also joined together and formed *landsmanshaften* and national political organizations. Local groups organized social and recreational activities, while each national group—the Federation of North African Immigrants, the Organization of Hungarian Immigrants, and so forth—sought to help its members in their negotiations with government and allied agencies.

An immigrant's sense of social solidarity was, therefore, with his fellow immigrants. Moreover, solidarity between immigrants was further emphasized by the popular practice of categorizing them according to their country of origin: they were referred to as 'Iraqis' or 'Cochinis', 'Hungarians' or 'Kurds'. These ethnic labels became part of an immigrant's sense of identity, and this, too, reinforced the bonds between them. The labels themselves have a certain irony: in their countries of origin the immigrants had all been 'Jews', but, in Israel, their Jewish identity faded into the background as each group adopted a new, ethnic affiliation. Only in Israel were they 'Moroccans' or 'Yemenites', for in their countries of origin they had never been considered to be true nationals. More important, each immigrant group was ranked within a society-wide social hierarchy: some were ranked high, others low, and therefore 'to be a Moroccan' or 'to be a Hungarian' made a great deal of difference. This point will shortly be elaborated upon. In brief, not only were immigrants drawn to one another, their new ethnic identity also had a crucial status meaning.

In addition to group ties, the immigrant experience also influenced the newcomers' family relations. There are, however, important differences in family structure between European and Middle Eastern immigrants, and the experience of each of these two groups must therefore be considered separately.

For Europeans, 'family' normally includes a comparatively narrow range of persons—wife and children, in-laws, grand-parents, aunts and uncles, some cousins. Family relations, among Europeans, form only one of many kinds of social ties and obligations, and not necessarily the most important one. Not so for Middle Easterners: although there is great diversity within this category, the term 'family' traditionally included a larger range of persons, and was more pivotal, than among Europeans. Middle Easterners expected *most* of the family, and family-oriented activities were extensive.

In the country of origin—in Iraq, Tripoli or Yemen—the patriarch was head of the family and wife and children were clearly subordinate. A kind of 'extended family' was usual, in which a father and his married sons lived with or near to one another; within this group the elder father and mother were the dominant figures, bearing authority and respect. Patterns of filial responsibility were drilled into the youth: tenderly dealt with while young, they were expected to support their parents in their old age. In addition to the family itself, relatives were also near at hand: cousin marriages were frequent, and these alliances further cemented the bonds between kinsmen. No other group could compare with the family: it was one's major affiliation.

34

Israeli conditions presented many difficulties which hindered the preservation of traditional ties. The male family heads shifted uneasily, if at all, into new occupational slots. Young people adapted much more quickly; they learned the new language, and in many instances they also became the major source of family income. Wives, too, found opportunities for greater independence: many women worked, and the veteran core culture also promoted a sense of feminine autonomy. How could a man remain 'patriarch' when he was himself confused, and when he came to depend upon his wife and children? The melancholy sight of a young girl interpreting for her father as they march between government offices—the elder uncomprehending, confused, the youngster bright-eyed, awed with her sudden responsibility—attests dramatically to the strains family relations underwent. The traditional authority patterns became weakened, or even broken down entirely: parents who were no longer able to control their family fortunes either drifted into sullen apathy, or became rigidly authoritarian in an effort by some means to recover their traditional control.

The uneven exposure to the new culture is a key element in this rupturing of family ties. Immigration inevitably widens the gap between generations: in Israel, just as in the United States or Australia, children quickly learn the new cultural style, while their parents are uncertain and cling to traditional behaviour. Conflicts naturally result from this cultural gap: fathers and sons misinterpret and misunderstand one another. In Israel, however, these difficulties were aggravated by the extraordinary efforts to 'capture' the immigrant youth: the movement for reform was primarily aimed at youngsters, and intensive efforts were made to develop a 'new spirit' among them. The model of the *sabra* became influential among some immigrant youngsters: at school, in youth groups or in the army they copied the modes of behaviour of the native-born. Their resocialization meant, in effect, Westernization: in the schools Yemenite and Iraqi boys studied European history and literature, and the model of behaviour presented to them in class was similarly Western. The army, itself a vast school for immigrant youth, reinforced this Western bent: separated from home and family, the recruits were encouraged to shed their old ways, and to adopt the traditions of their Israeli-born, Western-bred officers.

35

Inter-generational conflicts grew out of these different experiences. And yet, sharp as these conflicts are, when contrasted with the Europeans the Middle Eastern families still appear strong, even vibrant. European families, among which the inter-generational ties are comparatively brittle, seem to expect adolescent revolt, whereas among Middle Easterners familial expectations are greater, and family and kinsmen continue to represent deep emotional ties. In a recent study comparing European and Yemenite youngsters in a small Israeli town, the investigators were surprised to discover how powerful the Yemenite family ties were in contrast with the European: only 5 per cent of the European youngsters reported that they 'fully accept' parental authority, while 29 per cent of the Yemenites acknowledged 'full acceptance'.[5] In addition, among Middle Easterners variant forms of extended families are still common, and kinsmen, too, play vital functions in a wide range of situations. Even though the family roles are being re-defined, Middle Eastern family groups continue to be distinct, potent units.

These are important conclusions: if patterns of association largely follow ethnic lines, and if familial relations are also maintained, then a distinct sense of ethnic difference is likely to be transmitted between generations. Yemenite or Hungarian parents communicate something distinctively 'Yemenite' or 'Hungarian' to their children. On the one hand, as was emphasized earlier, common consumption patterns point to general similarities within the entire population. But, on the other hand, if family and ethnic traditions remain potent, the style with which these items are used, as well as the selections made, will differ from group to group. There is substantial evidence for such continuity. For example, food preferences differ widely between groups: Middle Easterners as a whole consume fewer dairy products than do Europeans, and each particular group follows its own eating habits. Expenditures for education are also different; Europeans as a group expend more funds on schooling than do Middle Easterners. To cite a more graphic instance, additions to the standard type of housing allocated to immigrants often shows the imprint of their traditions. The same structure will be modified differently by different groups; Europeans add on another room to the standard unit, while Middle Easterners often prefer to build a more spacious, enclosed courtyard. In these ways and others, the life styles of the various immigrant groups have an observable persistence.

These conclusions do not mean, of course, that immigrants have only an ethnic identification; in addition to that role they are also citizens, engage in political activities, have occupational responsibilities, participate in recreational activities, and so forth. Nor does it mean that the immigrants' traditions merely proceed untouched and unchanged—as we have already observed, their traditions often are altered. Moreover, the second-generation youngsters, those born in Israel, or those who spent their formative years there, tend to adopt new forms of thought and act. Yet, even with these changes—those already discussed, and those still to be described—ethnic-group associations, and ethnic traditions, define major blocs within Israeli society and culture.

We and They

Attention has thus far been focused upon intra-group ties. But what of the relations between members of different groups? And how do immigrants relate to the veteran dominated public agencies? These latter issues, a third dimension of the immigrant experience, are especially critical for understanding the immigrants' expressions of apathy, disaffection, commitment or ambivalence.

It is important to recognize, in the first place, that immigrants have a sense of Jewish affiliation with their new society. In the previous section, 'being Jewish' was described as 'fading' into the background, as ethnic affiliations crystallize and predominate. Certainly this occurs. And yet the Jewish bond, the Jewish identity, is also significant, and does influence behaviour. To be a Jew in a predominantly Jewish society is a new experience: whether they came from Syria or Czechoslovakia, the immigrants were formerly members of Jewish minorities, and they were to some extent restricted and withdrawn. There is, therefore, profound emotional satisfaction with their new majority status. It is emotionally pleasing to be 'at home', to sense and claim identification throughout the society. Religious holidays—the New Year, Passover, the weekly sabbath celebration—are occasions during which immigrants can unite with their new society: no matter whether they are religious or secular, during these moments their society-wide links are given vivid expression.

Nationalist identifications also unite the Jewish community. Just like the veterans, immigrants are keenly aware of being the first generation in a reborn Israel. They take pride in the new state's achievements, and they are proud, too, to be participants in historic, dramatic events. Israeli nationalism is a potent communal force: immigrants flock to Independence Day parades, and they respond enthusiastically to national symbols and national heroes. These Jewish ties and communal attachments are, no doubt, reinforced by the ever-present sense of external threat; the hostile borders, and recent memories of conflict and war. Yet the identification would be there in any case: notwithstanding the fact that immigration has powerfully strengthened, even created, a sense of cultural difference and ethnic identity, it has also led to a pervading sense of communal solidarity.

These sentiments do influence behaviour: no matter how different persons appear from one another, or how strange their customs seem to be, when they are perceived as Jews the bonds that unite them are stressed. This may limit violence: 'We disagree and argue, but after all, we are all Jews!' There is also a sense of propriety—of what is 'proper' behaviour between Jews—and this, too, acts to restrain excess and promote sympathetic understanding.

Yet, on the other hand, these communal claims themselves can become a source of frustration. Immigrants develop expectations regarding their new Jewish society. By and large, these are optimistic expectations: if an immigrant formerly expected rebuff or worse from a non-Jewish society, he naturally awaits warmth and understanding from a predominantly Jewish society. But alas! The expectations that are built up are bound to become disappointments. It is too much to expect that members of one's society will for ever (or even ever) behave in a warm, permissive fashion, so that when fellow-citizens respond not with sympathy, but rather with unconcern or worse, then the blow is doubly hard. It is not only that immigrants' information may be in error, or that they are confused; it is also, in many instances, that they expect and await kindness, and meet instead with a harsher social reality.

The ranking of ethnic groups is one cardinal source of frustration; that is, the prestige attached to ethnic-group membership provokes disaffection *on the parts of the lower-ranking groups*. As was earlier pointed out, an ethnic affiliation—to be a Yemenite, Hungarian or Tunisian—is also a status position: ethnic groups are ranked differentially, and belonging to one or another group has great social meaning. A person's name, his accent, the cut of his clothes, the shade of his skin—all of this (and more) is perceived, catalogued, and therefore reacted to.

The basis of ethnic stratification should by now be clear. As might be expected, the major prestige criterion is the similarity between the immigrants and the veteran European settlers. The closer the conformity, the higher the rank. Europeans, or to use the more common designation, *Ashkenazim*, are ranked higher than Middle Easterners, or *Sephardim*. To come from Poland or Britain is, *ipso facto*, to be more prestigious than to have one's origins in Egypt or Iraq. This rift is fundamental, and it runs throughout the society. There are, of course, gradations within each category. Yemenites, for example, seem to be ranked higher than Moroccans. Yemenites have an aura of exoticism: their rapid transition from feudal to modern conditions, as well as the folk arts some still retain, has focused interest upon them. More important, perhaps, is the popular reputation Yemenites have as 'good workers' and 'frugal persons': in these respects they conform to the European veterans' stress upon physical labour and personal simplicity. Moroccans, on the other hand, are considered to be excitable, dangerous and devoid of cultural attainments. ('Morocco-sakin', the knife-wielding Moroccan, is a popular stereotype.) Europeans are also ranked differentially: Yugoslavs, who are considered to have quickly adopted new occupations, are often called 'good material', while Rumanians, who may be concentrated in small-scale commerce, are stereotyped as grasping, sharp traders. But more important than these variations is the fact that, taken as a whole, to be of European descent is widely recognized as lending higher prestige. For example, research conducted in

39

an ethnically mixed housing project showed not only that Europeans in the project ranked highest, and Moroccans lowest, but also that the Moroccans concurred in grading themselves low and the Europeans high.[6]

It takes little imagination to see that this ranking must lead to resentment on the part of the lower-placed groups: the Middle Easterners. Having immigrated with such high hopes, it is deeply disturbing to discover that being 'Moroccan' or 'Iraqi' automatically sets one low in the social scale. Not only is there resentment, there is an even more powerful sense of discrimination: Middle Easterners are firmly convinced that they are discriminated against. There can be little doubt that these feelings are widespread, and that, whether real or imaginary, Middle Easterners believe that prejudice and discrimination are levelled against them. Why do Europeans live in the fashionable suburbs, and Middle Easterners in the slums? Why are Europeans chosen for the best posts—the better-paid jobs, or high-prestige positions? The answer is simple; because they are chosen by other Europeans. Preference (so it is felt by Middle Easterners) is always given to Europeans, while the least desirable places and positions are allotted to 'our people'. Other explanations may be proffered to explain the differences; for example, since Europeans as a group are better educated they have advantages in competition for many posts. Yet no matter how rational-sounding the explanation, the sense of discrimination persists. Moreover, there can be no doubt that some Europeans are indeed prejudiced; terms such as *shechorim*, 'the blacks', or *frankim*, are popular expressions of biased attitudes. These new immigrants, some of whom are dark-skinned, and most of whom possess different traditions, are disliked and feared by some. For their part, too, Middle Easterners speak of the disliked *vus-vus*—the European chattering in an incomprehensible Yiddish. There is no accurate survey of how widespread these feelings may be, or among which groups they are strongest. Discrimination is decried by all public groups—in recent years government directives have been issued giving preference to Middle Easterners—and there is strong moral pressure opposing prejudiced views. (A recently published near-racist book which extolled the 'Ashkenzic virtues' and decried the 'Sephardic backwardness' was publically condemned by the

Prime Minister.) And yet: the sense of discrimination persists, and it results in underlying tensions in group relations.

These tensions find expression in various ways. There is a strong sense of group consciousness—a 'we' and 'they' feeling—so that persons are responded to differently depending upon their origins. This does not necessarily indicate hostility, yet members of the different groups are often not fully at ease with one another. Another, very different expression of this tension is the attempt to escape a low-status position by forging a new ethnic identity. For example, some North Africans (who are generally regarded as low-ranking) may identify themselves as 'Frenchmen'. To be 'French' is preferable to being 'Moroccan', and so some deny their true origins and seek to adopt a higher, more respected ethnic label. This search for a higher status shows how emotionally trying the ethnic ranking can be; for surely this is a new form of self-hatred.

In addition to these responses, inter-group tensions have sometimes exploded in violence. Incidents of violence have not been widespread (the cohesive factors in the society are strong —'We are all Jews, we have so many enemies'), and yet they *have* occurred, and threaten to recur. The most explosive case of communal antagonism took place in 1959, when rioting broke out in several cities. The demonstrators were mainly North Africans: the street mobs—those who smashed store windows in Haifa and Beersheba—were verbally protesting against police brutality and their own bleak residential conditions. But mainly they were disappointed and frustrated by their low position, and angry and resentful against the society that neither sympathized with nor understood them. In brief, there is often an 'edge' to inter-group relations, and group consciousness is reinforced by antagonisms between Europeans and Middle Easterners.

There is also a second major source of frustration: namely, relations between immigrants and government agencies. Some overlap exists between these two—Europeans monopolize the higher government posts—but immigrant-bureaucrat ties go far beyond ethnicity, and involve different situations and different problems.

There are many reasons why immigrants must frequently come into contact with government officials. Most immigrants lack financial resources, and they depend upon public agencies for housing, employment or loans; national development programmes expand the scope of central direction and administrative control, and this too brings immigrants into frequent contact with officials; public groups (such as the Jewish Agency and Histadruth) had widespread economic power in the pre-state period, and since 1948 their activities have expanded; certain key resources—particularly food and housing—were sometimes in short supply, and they were therefore rationed or allocated by the government. For all of these reasons immigrants and government officials were frequently in contact with one another: an immigrant would register for work with the government employment service; he would often work in a public enterprise; housing would be allocated by the Jewish Agency; medical care would be provided in a Histadruth clinic, and so forth.

In addition to these reasons, the immigrant government-bureaucrat relationship became so prominent since officials wished to direct the immigrants towards achieving national goals. The immigrants pouring into the country were seen as a vehicle for carrying out public programmes; members of the veteran community were reluctant to become pioneers again —the 'crisis in pioneering' diminished the older, public spirit —so in their place immigrants were directed to areas deemed essential by government policy. Controlling immigration and settlement therefore meant a kind of 'bureaucratic absorption', in which state representatives directed and controlled key aspects of the immigrants' lives. The bureaucratic web therefore reached out into many situations, and the administrators' motives were also mixed.

Given this type of relationship, conflicts of interest between immigrants and bureaucrats were common. An immigrant, for example, might wish for a home in the centre of the country, near to his friends and close to work centres; but the settlement officials were interested in settling the northern and southern peripheries, and immigrants in tens of thousands were shipped to new towns and villages in those areas. In some instances wave after wave of immigrants was dispatched to some lonely town or village, in the hope that a few would remain and form the nucleus of a community. It was possible to leave, but leaving was always a tortuous process of negotiation, threat and argument. The housing authorities were constantly besieged by families wishing to be transferred from one place to another: demonstrations, hunger strikes and plain refusals to comply were commonplace. In much the same way, loans were available for certain kinds of enterprise, but not for others: the officials' priority-list determined which requests to support, and which to reject. For the immigrants, the choices appeared arbitrary and dictatorial. Immigrants were certainly being offered a great deal—homes, employment, job-training—but often these were things they did not desire.

These conflicts often had their roots in the discrepancy between the bureaucrats' socialist-reformist ideals, and the immigrants' utter indifference, or active opposition, to this ideology. Government administrators hoped to transform the immigrants—to induct them into co-operatives, or to make them into proud workers. For their part, the immigrants wished to retain their own traditions: to live as they pleased. Inevitably, this confrontation led to misunderstanding and confusion. For example, immigrants organized into farming co-operatives were allocated livestock and seeds with which to begin their agricultural career; but not wishing to become farmers, they sold their cows and traded the seed for meat or a radio. To the government administrator, this behaviour was immoral and shocking; yet what could be expected from the non-ideological immigrant? Some immigrants soon learned that the government bureaucracies could, if handled properly, be manipulated for their own benefit. For the administrator, these actions were yet another example of the newcomers' 'primitive mentality'. From the immigrants' perspective, however, this behaviour was perfectly reasonable: after all, the funds being expended were for immigrants, and shouldn't they simply pocket the money and do as they please? Misunderstandings were therefore present on all sides: it was only as more practical programmes were initiated (as has occurred in recent years) that greater consensus began to emerge.

In addition to conflicts of interest, the constant bickering with public agencies was itself frustrating. The task faced by the agencies was enormous (imagine providing housing for a population that doubled in three years!) and the growing new towns and villages attest to the planners' skill. And yet, over-whelmed by mass-immigration, government groups often func-tioned inefficiently. An immigrant in search of a job, home or insurance compensation was inevitably shunted from office to office, while the officials conferred, searched for his file, and then, frequently, passed the decision on to another committee. It is therefore hardly surprising that immigrants were frequently confused and angry. Then, too, since so many items were controlled administratively, cries of favouritism—*protekziah*—were continuously voiced. Real cases of graft or corruption were probably rare; but the suspicions were ever-present. Since most higher officials were Europeans, the Middle Eastern immigrants again felt disadvantaged: the Polish immigrant could converse with the official in Yiddish, but the Tunisian or Yemenite stood mute or incomprehending.

In time, with luck and moderate economic success, these contacts became less frequent: an immigrant with a home and permanent job—a 'settled immigrant'—was less dependent upon governmental agencies. Contacts between them and the bureaucracies was not appreciably different from the veteran Israelis. Many immigrants did not, however, become 'settled': the old and sick, or those who could not adjust to the rigours of their new life, continue to be dependent upon the national agencies. Moreover, each successive wave of immigrants met these problems anew. An immigrant from, say, Hungary or Morocco arriving in Israel in 1965 receives better accommoda-tion and more skilful treatment than did his cousin who immigrated ten years earlier: yet, just as their cousins did, the current crop of immigrants must also learn to cope with the national bureaucracies.

Ambivalence, Apathy, Disaffection and Commitment

These comments regarding the immigrant experience—the new consumption patterns, ethnic group organization, family strains or inter-group tensions—are of general importance in the analysis of Israeli society, and we will return to them again in subsequent chapters. But first, it is now possible to return to the problems posed at the beginning of this chapter: what factors produce ambivalence, apathy, disaffection or commitment among immigrants?

The preceding sections contain clues to ambivalence. Immigrants who have mastered new skills, and who have been able to acquire some of the strategic symbols of the veteran culture, are attracted to Israeli society. An immigrant who has, for example, risen to become a chief clerk in an office, or who has a permanent job in a construction gang, may fall into this category: he is likely to own an apartment, send some of his children to secondary school, have a newly acquired refrigerator and radio. In addition to economic success, immigrants are also pleased to be Jews in a Jewish society, and this, too, binds them to their new country.

There are, however, contradictory experiences. Economic success is, after all, a relative matter: immigrants may be 'better off', but comparing their own situation with that of others often leads to disappointment and frustration. Moreover, *entrée* to the élite pioneer or middle-class groups is not so much dependent upon income as upon acquiring the veteran European cultural style. The credentials for belonging, such as participation in pioneer movements, or friendships within the government establishment, are not easily acquired. These immigrants therefore have the sense of being an 'out-group': they are unable to enter the élite ranks. This, too, is inherently frustrating. Finally, even though the Jewish communal ties do attach immigrants to the society, the sense of discrimination felt by many Middle Easterners builds up resentment. How can one enthusiastically affirm one's allegiance to a society that discriminates against one's self and fellows? Ambivalence is the product of these contradictory impulses: it results from the clash between the immigrants' economic advantage and political security, and the strivings that are still unresolved plus the social bars that are resented.

Evidence of immigrant ambivalence is presented in Professor Eisenstadt's study, *The Absorption of Immigrants*. In considering a range of immigrant responses, Eisenstadt describes two types—the 'isolated stable family', and the 'cohesive traditional group'—that emphasize ambivalent feelings. The 'isolated stable family' includes immigrants who have successfully adopted new occupations, but who also feel themselves closed

off from wider social participation. These families have, Eisenstadt writes, 'a generally positive identification with the country
. . . [but] little orientation towards the general values of the
social system'.[7] In the type labelled 'cohesive traditional',
immigrants are disposed to adopt new occupations and economic skills, but they also express 'a strong element of aggression
towards the absorbing society and towards some of its central
aspects and values'.[8] Although hardly conclusive, Eisenstadt's
observations lend support to the presence of ambivalent feelings
among some immigrants.

The apathetic immigrants are those who are unable to find
meaning in their lives—those who draw little satisfaction from
their new occupations, and who are unable to link themselves
to the wider society in any meaningful fashion. Eisenstadt, who
has drawn up a lengthy description of this response, emphasizes
the fact that the apathetic 'had no coherent set of values by
which to organize their different roles', and consequently they
'constitute the marginal cases in the society'.[9] Confused by the
shock of the new, and unable to construct a satisfactory self-
image (to become a farmer, or to live in a remote town),
apathetic immigrants withdrew into themselves, and did not
enjoy close relations with either immigrants or veterans.

Apathy has various roots: unfulfilled expectations, an
inability to adjust to new occupations, or the corroding
influence of long-term dependence upon bureaucratic groups.
The numerous 'social cases'—persons publicly supported and
their families—probably fall into this category. Parents who do
not recover from the shock of lost authority, or who become
depressed by endless, unsuccessful negotiation with the bureaucracies, also become apathetic. Sapped of resolve by earlier
disappointment, they retreat to the margins and live without
long-term goals and plans.

Unlike the ambivalent (who have mixed emotions), or the
apathetic (who lack involvement), the disaffected bitterly dislike
their position: they reject the norms and conditions of their
new life, and rebel against them. This response has its source in
several conflict points. For example, an immigrant who refuses
to follow a new trade, or who rejects a home in a *moshav*, comes
into recurrent conflict with the national bureaucracies and often
emerges embittered and despairing. The youngsters who have

no marketable skills, who drift from one job to the next, or those who flee from the new towns and drift into urban slums —they, too, are among the disaffected. Prejudice is another root-cause: prejudice produces a frustrating sense of exclusion, and frustrations spill over into total rejection of the society. Finally, immigrants whose expectations were particularly high —for example, former Zionist leaders—are sometimes disillusioned by their Israeli experience. The latter came with high hopes: but the often harsh reality was especially shocking for them, and some become excessively critical and withdrawn.

Attitudes such as these are found among all immigrant groups: Yemenites and Poles, Hungarians and Germans. Yet it is likely that disaffection is more prominent among Middle Eastern immigrants. They have few of the economic skills necessary to making a positive adjustment, and the prejudice they sense drives them away from the society's core. The Wadi Salib street mobs, or the angry demonstrators protesting in front of government offices, are vivid examples of disaffection. Beyond such sporadic outbursts, the general sense of being an 'out-group' also leads to this response. Nissim Rejwan, a Middle Eastern journalist, writes that 'members of this deprecated community have come to refuse to have any truck with their cultural "superiors", and seem to have resigned themselves to a state of permanent separation'.[10]

And the committed? The committed associate themselves with the élite groups, and affirm the new society's values and viewpoints. These are the immigrants who successfully follow the pioneer or middle-class model. The committed find new meaning in their lives, and take pleasure in the new activities they perform. Rather than withdrawing because of prejudice, they find comradeship and warmth; instead of difficult occupational crises, they discover new opportunities. The youngsters who have responsible positions in the regular army, immigrants actively engaged in local politics, or the former Zionist leader who finds a niche in one of the national agencies: these are all examples of committed immigrants. To a considerable extent they have adopted the manners and values of the élite groups: their patterns of speech, dress and deportment are successfully modelled after the veteran Europeans. For this reason many of the committed are found among the younger immigrants: they, after all, have many advantages in adapting to the new society. Committed immigrants no doubt include members of all immigrant groups—Middle Easterners as well as Europeans—and they therefore compose a broad spectrum of the immigrant population.

These generalizations regarding the immigrant population are, to be sure, speculative. The data upon which they are based are incomplete, and some of the studies (such as Professor Eisenstadt's) were done more than a decade ago. For these reasons the response categories must be considered to be tentative: additional research is needed in order to confirm the prevalence of an 'ambivalent response', or, indeed, to determine whether the typology itself is useful. While the speculative nature of the categories should be borne in mind, the available empirical data, as well as more impressionistic sources, do lend support to the typology developed in this chapter.

It should also be recalled that the response categories are conceived of as alternating states of mind: as new potentials are uncovered, or new types of relations entered into, the immigrants' response also changes. There is undoubtedly a shift both towards and away from the extremes of commitment and disaffection, just as moods of apathy and ambivalence also vary. While for some these responses are permanent, for most 'ambivalence' or 'disaffection' is of brief duration.

To understand the conditions that give rise to these responses is essential for interpreting inter-group relations. In order to complete the analysis, however, these short-term, fluctuating responses need to be considered together with longer-range developments. Some of these 'secular trends'— the now crystallizing social forms—are considered in the next chapter.

4

PATTERNS OF MOBILITY

THE prevailing patterns of Israeli society and culture are new, and they have also changed dramatically in the period since the state's formation. This rapidity of change poses hazards for social research: since social and economic conditions change quickly, a 'snap-shot' analysis of group relations soon grows out of date. The discussion in the last chapter of changes in occupation, or relations with Israel's officialdom, focused upon such short-term situations. It is also necessary to consider longer-range developments. What social trends can be identified in the seventeen years since the state's formation? Have group relations crystallized and thereby assumed a characteristic form?

One important long-range issue is the question of immigrant social mobility. Social mobility, or the extent to which individuals and groups rise or fall in prestige and power in relation to others, is a decisive issue in any study of immigrant-absorption. Mobility is so important since, as a rule, the more upward-mobile immigrants are likely to become rapidly absorbed. Conversely, those who 'rise' slowly, or are frozen into a low position, retain their traditional cultural features over longer periods of time. There are good reasons why this should be the case. The immigrants' chances of attaining better-paid jobs, or moving into more prestigeful neighbourhoods, depend upon their ability to perform like the veterans. As new roles are made available to them, in work, politics or informal cliques, immigrants adopt the behavioural characteristics of the veteran society. To put it differently: their ethnic identity is replaced by a class identity, and they thereby become not so

49

much 'immigrants', or the sons of immigrants, as members of a social class. On the other hand, a failure to 'rise'—concentrating in low-paid occupations, or congregating in the old, densely-packed neighbourhoods—reinforces the old ties and traditional customs, and does not lead to rapid absorption. This pattern is, of course, not inevitable: under certain circumstances a group may rise in wealth or education without adopting many of the habits of those around them. But these are special cases: the usual pattern in Western societies is for mobility to be associated with social and cultural assimilation.

Mobility can be measured in different ways; indeed, the measures vary according to the criteria considered desirable in the society being studied. Income, place of residence, attendance at élite schools, or membership of prestige groups (in America, the 'country-club set', or the banking and heavy-industry élites) are among the measures that have been used for determining the relative positions of different groups, and for assessing how their positions change over time. In the case of Israel, it is important to recognize that the duality between 'pioneer' and 'middle-class' models presents immigrants with alternative mobility routes. Although there is some overlap between the two—organizational skills are desirable in both *kibbutz* and commercial enterprises—to an important degree different criteria exist in the two sectors. For example, an immigrant who joins a border settlement immediately becomes part of a prestigeful group; or a flair for leadership may open new avenues for immigrants in *kibbutz* or *kibbutz*-linked groups. On the other hand, in the middle-class sector, 'rising' depends upon income, education or political skills. It may therefore be seen that, depending upon the route chosen, the process of mobility becomes different for immigrants. However, the great majority of immigrants follow the middle-class model: few have joined *kibbutzim* or become involved in other pioneer-type groups, while the majority by far pursue middle-class interests. Immigrants have become unskilled or semi-skilled workers, or they continue to follow craft or commercial interests. The usual ambitions are to rise to higher positions—to become a higher-graded clerk, be promoted to foreman, own a larger store, and so forth. In brief, although competing models are present in the society, it is the middle-class ladder that most immigrants seek to climb. For this reason the analysis developed in this chapter pertains chiefly to immigrants within the middle-class sector.

Four indices have been selected as mobility-measures in Israeli society: income, education, marriage and politics. By using these gauges one can see how the various groups in the society stand in relation to each other, and how their relative positions change over time. Income and education statistics disclose whether immigrants are concentrated in particular occupational slots, and what their future positions are likely to be. Marriage statistics are also important: by analysing the prevalence of marriage between groups one obtains an index to primary-group assimilation. Political participation is another crucial gauge; it reveals the extent to which immigrants have penetrated into the 'Israeli establishment'. These criteria are, therefore, especially sensitive: they reveal a great deal regarding the extent of mobility, and assimilation, in Israeli society.

Income Distribution: Who Gets What?

The distribution of income, or, more specifically, how the incomes of different groups stand in relation to one another, is a critical index of mobility. Consumption items—a car, apartment, refrigerator, stylish clothes—do symbolize a person's rank. Income depends upon occupation, and occupations are ranked differentially: the 'white-collar' positions of administrators, professionals or executives are generally preferred over the working-man's 'blue-collar' occupations. (To a considerable extent this is equally true of the 'pioneer sector'.) Income is also self-perpetuating: the well-to-do families can afford the heavy expense of sending their children through high-school and university, and their children's careers are therefore well launched. Income does, then, provide an index of mobility. To cite several examples, mobility is exemplified by the immigrant who, beginning as a minor official in a government office, subsequently becomes the head of an administrative district; or the *moshav* member who, from modest beginnings, now owns a substantial dairy herd; or the shopkeeper in a new town who has prospered over the years.

Fortunately, Giora Hanoch's study of 'Income differentials in Israel' provides an excellent analysis of this dimension of mobility.[1] Drawing upon data collected in 1951, 1954, 1957 and 1960, Hanoch is able not only to show differentials in income, but also to chart how these have changed over time. Hanoch takes note, first of all, of the high degree of economic egalitarianism that characterizes Israeli society: in comparison with Sweden, West Germany, the Netherlands, Great Britain or the United States, the Israeli urban population is characterized by a narrow range of income distribution. There are no great, dramatic disparities in income: for example, there is no Israeli landed gentry or industrialist class, and the aged, ill or poverty-stricken are cared for by the appropriate national welfare agencies. Not only are the extremes muted, the real income of the entire population has risen dramatically in the past decade and a half. This point was made earlier: all segments of the population have benefited from Israeli economic development. These two points—the general rise in income, and the society-wide economic egalitarianism—should be kept in mind while examining the important differences in income that do exist.

For Hanoch's study shows conclusively that the incomes of different groups in the population have climbed unequally: indeed, a major conclusion of his study is that although the extremes are narrow, *Israeli society exhibits a growing inequality in income.* For example, in 1950 the disposable income (income after taxes) of the bottom 50 per cent of wage-earners amounted to 40·1 per cent of total income, and the top half 59·9 per cent —while in 1956–7 the bottom half included only 35·1 per cent, and the top half received 64·9 per cent.[2] (These figures, and those given subsequently, refer to urban wage and salary earners; although they are therefore incomplete, Hanoch believes that including rural segments would only tend to increase the degree of inequality.) This growth of inequality (a trend that runs counter to the recent experience of most Western countries) may be due to several factors: income inequality during the crisis years following the state's establishment was exceedingly narrow, and the subsequent removal of wage-controls and rationing produced increased inequality. More important, mass-immigration changed the entire structure of the society, and since the incoming flood of immigrants were concentrated in the bottom-income groups, they thereby produced greater inequality in the society as a whole.

Income distribution in Israeli society shows increasing inequality. But the crucial question is: which groups benefit the most? Which incomes rise quickly, and which rise slowly or not at all?

Hanoch's analysis concentrates upon two key comparisons: immigrants *versus* veterans, and Europeans *versus* Middle Easterners. His conclusions are meticulously arrived at, and convincing: 'First of all, the longer the period of residence in Israel of any group the higher its income . . . Secondly . . . persons of Oriental [Middle Eastern] origin have lower incomes, while persons from the West, as well as native-born children of European families, have higher ones.'[3] These are important conclusions, and they merit careful consideration.

In regard to veteran-immigrant incomes, the analysis demonstrates that veterans have much higher incomes than immigrants, and that, although the ratios vary, the income gap tends to grow wider with time. Table IV illustrates this tendency: in 1954 the ratio of incomes of pre-1931 veterans to post-1952 immigrants was 109 : 60; whereas by 1958 it grew to 106 : 41. Put in terms of monthly incomes, in 1954 the pre-1931 veterans earned an average of IL286, and the post-1954 immigrants IL154, while four years later the figures were IL381 and IL146.

TABLE IV

Index of Relative Income
by Period of Immigration[4]

Period of Inquiry	Period of Immigration					
	pre-1931	*1932–8*	*1939–47*	*1948–9*	*1950–1*	*post-1952*
1951	99	100	89	76	72	—
1954	109	100	86	74	72	60
1956–7	98	100	88	76	71	60
1957–8	106	100	91	70	61	41

How can this gap be explained? Veterans have obvious advantages over immigrants: they possess all of the skills necessary to achieve higher incomes: a knowledge of Hebrew, better mercantile positions, intimate ties to the national bureaucracies, strategic positions of economic control. Moreover, since skills ripen over time, veterans have the advantage of lengthy work-experience, while newcomers typically are obliged to adopt new occupations in which they are unskilled and perform inefficiently. These advantages contribute to the growing discrepancy in income. However, in order to understand the income gap properly the categories need to be further refined. The category 'post-state immigrant' masks the preponderance of Middle Easterners who immigrated during that period. In other words: the veteran-immigrant income-gap is also part of the contrast between Europeans and Middle Easterners, and it needs to be seen in those terms.

The analysis of income according to period of immigration and ethnic group (as shown in Table V) is especially revealing. This analysis demonstrates that Europeans consistently have higher incomes than Middle Easterners: matching the groups in each category—veteran Europeans *versus* veteran Middle Easterners, or new-immigrant Europeans *versus* new-immigrant Middle Easterners—shows that the Middle Easterners always fall below the Europeans.

TABLE V

Personal Family Income by
Continent of Origin and Period of Migration[5]
(IL per month)

Period of Inquiry and continent	Veteran (pre-1947)	New Immigrant (post-1948)	Israel-born
1951:			
Asia-Africa	71·0	62·9	—
Europe-America	85·7	65·7	—
1956–7:			
Asia-Africa	237·4	206·6	261·7*
Europe-America	322·9	259·2	324·7*
1959–60:			
Asia-Africa	381·4	259·6	—
Europe-America	478·2	343·3	—

* By father's continent of birth.

This pattern is also repeated among the Israeli-born: although youngsters born in Israel of Middle Eastern parents have higher incomes than either veteran or immigrant Middle Easterners, their income falls well beneath that of Israeli-born youngsters whose parents are Europeans. Hanoch has also computed income figures by country of origin: among Middle Easterners, Yemenites have the lowest incomes, North Africans the second-lowest and immigrants from Iraq-Iran the highest; among Europeans, immigrants from the Balkans have lower incomes than those from Poland and Russia. Yet the income of the *lowest* European group is higher than the most affluent Middle Easterners'.

These statistics apply to family income. Family size differs widely between Europeans and Middle Easterners: families in the latter group are 60 per cent larger than those in the former. Thus the income gap widens even further when measured in terms of personal income, and the living standard of Europeans and Middle Easterners draws even further apart.

Returning to Table V, a comparison of the incomes of veterans and immigrants from Europe shows the reverse trend: although the incomes of European immigrants fall below those of European veterans, they are close to (and in 1956-7 even surpassed) the incomes of veteran Middle Easterners. Indeed, a comparison of incomes according to occupation shows the following rank-order: European veterans, European immigrants, Middle Eastern veterans, Middle Eastern immigrants. In this case ethnicity is more significant than length of time in Israel. These findings, therefore, indicate that the incomes of European immigrants have risen more quickly than Middle Easterners: Europeans as a group are more mobile than their Middle Eastern brethren.

What accounts for the Middle Eastern–European income gap? Differences in occupation and education seem to be most important. The heavy concentration of Europeans in professional and executive posts, and Middle Easterners in unskilled and semi-skilled work, accounts for part of the income difference; so too do the higher educational attainments of Europeans. Thus when the incomes of European professionals are matched against Middle Eastern professionals, or European high-school graduates against Middle Eastern high-school graduates, the differentials narrow considerably. Yet even then disparities remain: the salaries of Yemenite or Iraqi clerks approach that of their European counterparts; taken as a group, however, they fall consistently beneath the Europeans. For this reason Hanoch concludes that, in addition to such

55

'objective factors' as occupation and education, other 'subjective' variables also play a part. Discrimination may explain the fact that unskilled workers or executives from Middle Eastern countries have lower incomes than Europeans in analogous positions: prejudice may block the Middle Easterner's path, or the Europeans' better-placed contacts lend them advantages in competing for higher posts.

These conclusions regarding income differentials should not be startling, for they were foreshadowed in the discussion in Chapter 2. What is surprising, however, is that the income gap tends to grow even wider over time: the trend is for the ethnic-income split to expand, rather than recede. To quote Hanoch:

> Whereas the relative situation of all families of Asian and African origin worsened in the period between 1951 and 1960, and their average income declined from 89 per cent to 76 per cent of the over-all average, there was an improvement in the relative situation of families from Europe and America . . . The benefits of the rise in real income therefore went in large measure to families of European and American origin . . . while the average real income of wage and salary earners of African and Asian origin rose at a much slower rate.[6]

Middle Easterners are not 'catching up' with their European peers; rather, they fall farther behind. They do not rise into middle- or high-income posts, but rather remain in the lower-paid positions. Some individuals, of course, may and do rise; but as a group they do not appear to be climbing rapidly. In a word: the income differentials between Europeans and Middle Easterners strongly suggest a class division, with Europeans predominating in higher-income, higher-class positions. There is no total 'freezing' of mobility—the European immigrants certainly do rise—and yet, over time, the ethnic division begins to approximate to a class stratification. This joining of ethnicity with class is extremely important: if it persists, it is certain to influence the future shape of the society.

Before pursuing this point further, however, it is useful to examine the situation in education. Income and education are closely allied, and it is helpful to consider them together.

Education and Ethnicity

Although there is some disagreement among specialists as to how essential education is for social mobility, there is general agreement that education provides one of the key ladders to higher status positions. How do the various segments of the Israeli population rank in terms of education?

Here, too, vivid differences exist between Europeans and Middle Easterners. Europeans as a group receive substantially more higher education than Middle Easterners: a much higher proportion of European youngsters go on to attend high-school and university. The statistics in this regard are quite clear. Whereas Middle Eastern children (that is, those born in Middle Eastern countries, or children born in Israel whose parents are Middle Eastern immigrants) compose 60 per cent of the primary-school population, their participation drops to 38 per cent in high-school and to only 5 per cent at university level. The differentials are overwhelming: higher education in Israel is nearly a European monopoly.

Moreover, not only is it the case that school attendance differs between these groups; the quality of their training is probably also different. Most schools in immigrant areas—in the development towns or new villages where Middle Easterners predominate—are not nearly on a par with schools in the veteran sections of the cities or in the veteran *kibbutzim* and *moshavim*: although there are some exceptional schools in immigrant areas, in general their teaching staff and facilities fall far below those in the cities. Since promotion to high-school or university is based upon performance in competitive national examinations, the students from immigrant areas are therefore at a disadvantage in comparison with others. These problems further increase the educational gap.

These marked differences in higher education need to be explained. Lower income is one factor: since Middle Eastern families have lower incomes than Europeans, children are often forced to begin working rather than continue their studies. Secondary school education is only in part government financed; the high tuition fees force Middle Eastern children to drop out, while their European peers, who can better afford the costs, continue in school. The government has recently provided extensive scholarship funds for Middle Eastern students, and this will undoubtedly close part of the educational gap. However, in addition to these cost factors, cultural differences also select against Middle Eastern students. As was pointed out earlier, the school curriculum is heavily slanted towards European traditions; the teachers are also predominantly European, and this too may give advantages to European students. Moreover, European families place great emphasis upon education, while among some Middle Eastern groups formal education is a relatively new experience, and the youngsters tend to lack family support. European students, therefore, experience little discontinuity between home and school, while, in contrast, Middle Eastern youngsters must vault over substantial barriers. These factors have also contributed to the lower educational participation of Middle Eastern youngsters.

The relevance of these differences for mobility should be clear: the 'mobility potential' of Middle Eastern young people is limited by their lower rate of secondary-school and university attendance. Increasingly, the better posts depend upon advanced training; Israel's economic future in large part rests upon a much larger development in science and technology, so that occupation and income will in the future depend even more heavily upon highly specialized skills. The 'education gap' therefore reinforces the 'income gap': this circular chain of circumstance serves to maintain, and possibly to deepen, the split between the groups.

Marriage Patterns: Who Marries Whom?

Education provides one important ladder by which persons sometimes rise in their society. Marriage is another way of moving from a lower to a higher position. A 'good marriage'— a union with a higher-status spouse—raises up the bride or groom to the mate's rank. Moreover, marriage between members of different groups often breaks down social and cultural barriers between them: the new couple, their children, and their families as well, all enter into new social relations, and these new ties may narrow the distance between them.

It may seem odd to call marriage between Jews 'intermarriage': after all, both partners in the marriage are Jewish.

And yet, the union of, say a Moroccan boy with a Polish girl, or a Yemenite girl with an Israeli-born lad whose parents are from Russia, does represent marriage between two distinct groups: the traditions of bride and groom, and certainly of their parents, are different, so that the label 'intermarriage' is appropriate. Middle Eastern–European unions may well be a path to mobility, and they certainly are a significant meeting-ground for members of each group. Indeed, much emphasis has been placed upon marriages of this type (the Tel Aviv municipality has even awarded a prize to 'mixed' couples!) since the opinion is commonly voiced that intermarriage is the best, most effective way to arrive at true group-mixing.

In Israel, couples who apply to be married fill out a rather detailed questionnaire, so that the gross figures for marriage between groups are quite precise. In 1960, 14·5 per cent of all marriages were between Europeans and Middle Easterners, while 85 per cent were marriages within each group. Unfortunately, these figures have not been broken down further: it is not clear whether some groups (for example, Tunisians or Hungarians) intermarry more frequently then others. However, a further analysis of the figures does reveal that the most common type of intermarriage takes place between a European groom and a Middle Eastern bride: there are twice as many marriages of this type as of the reverse kind. Apparently, it is more acceptable for a European male to marry a Middle Eastern female, than it is for a Middle Eastern male to marry a European female.

What do these marriage statistics reveal regarding mobility? Actually, they tell relatively little: the extent to which intermarriage is a vehicle for mobility cannot be deduced from these bare figures. More information must be available about the couples—for example, the bride's and the groom's educational background, or the social status of the parents—before evaluating the marriages in terms of mobility. (Veteran-immigrant marriages may also signify mobility, but again, the data are inadequate to provide conclusions.) The prevalence of European male–Middle Eastern female marriage does suggest, however, that there may be a mobility factor in some inter-marriages. If it is assumed that the new couple adopts the social position and status of the *husband*, then this form of

59

marriage may be a mobility ladder for brides, who are 'raised' to their husband's higher status. Marriage between a Middle Eastern groom and a European bride would not have this effect, and it may be for this reason that this kind of marriage is chosen less often. This is still in the realm of conjecture, however: more detailed information is needed in order properly to interpret these statistics.

Although the mobility function of marriage is still not clear, the marriage statistics do show that a sizeable minority marry members of different ethnic groups. Nearly one out of every six marriages is of this type, so that, to some extent at least, marriage does forge links between the two major social blocs. Moreover, the frequency of intermarriage appears to be slowly rising: the actual number of marriages of this type climbs from year to year, although the relative incidence of intermarriage grows more slowly.[7] Should this tendency quicken, then the number of intermarried couples would be substantial indeed. Such a development—were it to take place—might go far towards breaking down divisions between groups. Whether or not this will occur is, of course, far from certain. In the meantime, the preponderance of 'in-group' marriage—the 85 per cent who marry members of their own ethnic group—suggests that ethnic divisions are being reinforced by marriage. The pattern of Yemenite marrying Yemenite, Moroccan marrying Tunisian, or Hungarian marrying Israeli of European parentage, tends to maintain each group's traditions, and thereby retains their separate identity. If, as was suggested in the last chapter, Middle Eastern families retain their vibrancy, and if their children also marry other Middle Easterners, then substantial portions of their cultural traditions are likely to be transmitted from generation to generation. Ultimately, marriage between groups may lead to greater social and cultural fusion; at present, however, the selections in marriage tend more to reinforce the existing social distinctions.

The Political Road

Thus far we have considered income, education and marriage as factors in immigrant social mobility. Political participation is yet another potential index of mobility: by gaining access to elective or appointive posts, immigrants are able to rise to positions of higher prestige. The political avenue may, in fact, be particularly critical. In other societies formed by mass immigration, politics did provide a way for immigrants to rise. This is especially striking in the United States, where, during the past fifty years or so, the emergence of Irish, Italians, Jews and others to political prominence has signalled the general rise in status of ethnic minorities. In addition, the very structure of Israeli society emphasizes politics: with national institutions so dominant, and political parties so influential, politics may be an especially important mobility-ladder. For both of these reasons it is important to examine closely the relations between politics and social mobility.

One mobility path may begin with immigrant involvement in politics on a local level. If immigrants concentrate in particular areas—in cities, provinces or regions—then by dint of their sheer numbers they may 'capture' the local constituency. Although highly simplified, this seems to have been the classic pattern in the United States. In the United States, the heavy concentration of Irish in Boston, or Poles in Chicago, led to the election of Irish or Polish candidates in those cities. In turn, these public triumphs raised the prestige of the ethnics as a group, and also gave new economic advantages to other Irish or Poles. Immigrant strength on a local level also had national significance: whoever 'controlled' Chicago had a voice in selecting the governor of Illinois, and, ultimately, the President as well. In this way the ethnic politicians gained *entrée* to wider circles of power; and their rise to power and fame was also a rise for their constituents.

There are still other ways in which immigrants become politically mobile. For example, wealth may be a pre-condition for political mobility; only when ethnics are able to contribute substantially to the party do they influence the choice of candidates. Of course, political genius, sheer talent and administrative ability are also prime ingredients in political mobility— in addition to being 'ethnics' the candidates or organizers obviously must have substantial talent and skill.

Politics have, to some extent, become a means by which immigrants in Israel rise to higher positions: immigrants—both

61

Europeans and Middle Easterners—are politically active, and their weight is increasingly felt. Local factory committees or political party branches include many immigrants; indeed, these bodies provide an important framework for contact between different segments of the population. Several immigrants have also become town mayors, and others hold high administrative positions. It is also likely that immigrant participation in politics has increased over time; although this question has not been studied systematically, in comparison with, say, 1955, immigrants today are probably more active and hold down more positions. *Nevertheless, even though immigrants are active politically their influence, both as individuals and as groups, is still negligible. Immigrants have not been able to control important areas of power, nor have they been able to rise to truly influential positions. The politically-powerful posts—membership in party central committees, in parliament or the cabinet, high-level army command, or positions of trust in the reigning bureaucracies—are dominated by veterans (particularly European veterans), and few immigrants have as yet been able to move into these key slots.*

There are many reasons why immigrants have not yet reached higher political positions. The most obvious, of course, is that they are still immigrants: immigrants are, *ipso facto*, 'outsiders', and time is required before they can become political spokesmen. Control over government is the most sensitive social issue, and immigrants may not yet be sufficiently 'legitimate' for the electorate to entrust them with national leadership. On the other hand, however, immigrants are the *majority* in Israeli society: their majority position should find expression in politics. As was pointed out earlier, immigrants are concentrated in many towns and villages, and they predominate in scores of neighbourhoods. The veterans may not support them—but certainly the local immigrant concentrations might give them their support. Why, then, have immigrants not yet risen to important positions?

The answer to this paradox may be found in the special conditions of Israeli political life: namely that local politics are relatively unimportant, while national politics are well developed and highly centralized. Even though immigrants may rise to new positions on a local level they do not thereby enter politically significant posts, while the veteran European groups, who firmly control both the parties and the administrative bureaucracies, are able to monopolize the politically strategic positions. (The 'veteran leadership' includes both the older, pre-state leaders and the younger generation either born or reared in Israel. There are sharp conflicts within this élite group, but ethnicity is not an issue, since they are overwhelmingly Europeans.)

The comparative weakness of local political positions stems from several factors. In the first place, Israel's small size inhibits the growth of localism: when Tel Aviv is only hours away from immigrant-centres such as Beersheba or Kiryat Shmona, this physical proximity limits purely local attachments and instead favours the growth of national consciousness and national élites. Smallness in scale also means that national figures are well known throughout the society: a Ben Gurion, Beigin or Dayan are popular figures, and they inevitably tower over local city or village officials. As a consequence, local elections are often influenced by the national leadership: the voters, and these are immigrant voters, may choose the national leaders' party irrespective of its record in local affairs.

Not only are national figures dominant; economic power is concentrated in national institutions rather than in local groups. This tendency towards centralization obviously checks the development of meaningful local politics. Political and economic centralization has grown for several reasons. Once again, smallness in scale favours centralization—the system may be clumsy, but it apparently is possible to direct local affairs from Tel Aviv. Moreover, programmes of national economic development inevitably emphasize central planning and allocation. In Israel, where social as well as economic development has been planned by government groups, the tendencies towards centralization are strong. All decisions of any importance are made 'higher-up': a neighbourhood, *moshav* or town is a place from which requests are conveyed to national authorities, who then make decisions regarding an incredibly diverse range of issues. Local officials therefore have little to give away. Deprived of real power, and overwhelmed by national figures, meaningful local loyalties cannot develop.

There are still other reasons why localism has not prospered. Ever since the colonization period, and certainly in the post-1948 years, the critical political issues have all been national, rather than local or regional. Defence and economic development, the two major problems facing the Israeli polity, are eminently national issues. The municipal sewer system, or the local high-school, pale in importance before questions of national survival or taxation policies. Finally, the Israeli electoral system is also heavily weighted against localism. Elections in Israel are determined by proportional representation: each party submits a national list of candidates, and the number chosen depends upon the proportion of the total vote received by the party. In this system there are no 'senators', and no one 'stands for a seat' in any constituency. There are, in fact, no separate constituencies, but rather the nation as a whole represents a single constituency. No system could better frustrate any sense of local tie or local representation.

The total effect of all of these factors—small size, dominant national figures, economic centralization, accenting national issues, the electoral system—is to downgrade the influence of local politics. (Where localism is significant, in Tel Aviv or Haifa, to cite the prominent cases, the local party groups are veteran-dominated, and they are tightly linked to the national political hierarchy.) Local politics have not served as a springboard by which immigrants are able to attain prominence. Many have joined the major political parties: Mapai (the leading social-democratic party), the National Religious party, and Herut, a more militant, right-of-centre group, include substantial numbers of immigrants. Local party branches are in many instances composed of immigrants. Nevertheless, all of the major parties are led by members of the veteran European élite: there is a virtual veteran monopoly of power at national level, and in the several larger, more important local centres as well. Moreover, since the political parties control the key national institutions—the government, Jewish agency and Histadruth—leadership in these groups is also retained by veterans. Key posts in the ministries, or the leadership of national unions, are entirely in the hands of this group. Immigrant leaders, be they Yemenites, Moroccans or Hungarians, are not yet members of this reigning inner core. As yet they lack the common experiences, even the language, of the political élite, so that they are not socially acceptable to those who are truly 'on the inside'. Of course, the time is still brief, and the experience immigrants have at a lower level may be useful preparation for eventual political leadership. At least until now, however, immigrants have not arrived at political roles of major importance.

Frustrated by this situation, some immigrants—particularly Middle Easterners—have sought to organize separate national political parties. In the past, however, the ethnic parties have failed; they attract few voters in either national or local contests. The reasons for their failure are again related to the down-grading of local politics: the national parties are powerful and can offer substantial benefits, while the ethnic groups are weak, poorly supported and offer little materially to their constituents. Moreover, in competition with national leaders the ethnic politicians are clearly 'out of their class', and they have been defeated overwhelmingly. Until now, political separatism has not been an effective means of political mobility.

How Much Mobility?

We may now return to the questions raised at the beginning of this chapter: what conclusions can be drawn regarding mobility in Israeli society? To what extent have immigrants been able to rise to higher positions? What long-term trends can be identified?

There is, of course, a great deal of unevenness in mobility: as expected, some groups rise more rapidly than others. It seems clear that the major distinction is between Europeans and Middle Easterners: the incomes of European immigrants rise more rapidly, and their children also receive more advanced educational training. This rise in income and education draws the immigrant Europeans closer to the veterans, whereas, on the other hand, Middle Easterners are still sharply differentiated from the veteran Europeans. To put it differently: European immigrants rise more quickly to middle-class positions, where they meet and may merge with the veteran Europeans, while Middle Easterners rise slowly, or not at all. These class differences are expressed in important ways by separate residential areas, or different occupations. The class distinctions also support differences in life-style: so long as Middle Easterners are less mobile they may be expected to retain aspects of their traditional cultural patterns. This analysis of income and education therefore suggests that the cultural separation within Israeli society will persist so long as it is also a separation into classes.

The marriage statistics also support this conclusion. Most marriages are within the group, and they therefore reinforce the distinctions between groups. Any dramatic increase in the rate of intermarriage probably also depends upon higher incomes and better education among Middle Easterners. If members of these two groups were to share similar living standards—live in the same neighbourhoods, attend the same schools, have analogous occupations—then the rate of marriage between groups would probably also rise. Such a trend would undoubtedly provide a much deeper social and cultural interchange between them.

Many observers of the Israeli scene have taken the view that education holds the key to greater mobility for the Middle Eastern majority. This is a reasonable position, and government policy has recently aimed at raising the educational levels of Middle Easterners. For example, many immigrant children (primarily Middle Easterners) now attend an extra year of kindergarten, the length of their school day has been extended, and substantial scholarship funds have been made available to cover high-school tuition fees. These are all progressive policies, and they may enable more children to receive a higher education. In addition to such administrative reforms, however, changes in educational policy may also be required if the programme is to succeed. So long as these children are approached as if they were Europeans, the students are unlikely to perform well. For example, children are given heavy doses of homework on the assumption that their parents will assist them: this may succeed with Europeans, but it is unlikely to bear fruit with Middle Eastern parents who often do not know the language well, or who are themselves untutored in the intricacies of algebra or European history. Similarly, approaching these children as if their own cultural heritage were empty will also not lead to the desired results.

These conclusions regarding mobility pertain mainly to the

European–Middle Eastern split. The analysis of political mobility, however, suggests a continued cleavage between immigrants and veterans as entire groups. Immigrant Europeans may be somewhat more mobile in politics—it is difficult to arrive at precise comparative rates of political mobility— but, in general, veterans continue to dominate the political scene, while immigrants fill secondary positions. Although this may be the natural course of events, it is particularly vexing for some immigrants, and especially for Middle Easterners. Immigrants from Middle Eastern countries have been particularly sensitive to exclusion from major political posts, and they have increasingly turned against the established political parties. It should not be thought that this interest in political representation is mainly a desire for spoils: far from that, political representation in high places is a means to becoming legitimate, to firmly attaching one's self to the nation. A Yemenite minister, or a Moroccan judge, are, in themselves, evidence that these groups have 'arrived'. This is what Middle Easterners want: some tangible indication that they, too, 'belong'. As yet, their disaffection has not crystallized around support for purely Middle Eastern parties (as was mentioned earlier, these groups have not found wide support) but it may, in the future, either take that course or even swing to the support of more extreme groups. The extent of future political mobility may therefore be a key to the unfolding of inter-group relations.

These last comments indicate—finally—that the 'mobility gaps' may add fuel to the latent tensions between ethnic groups. It is unlikely that Middle Easterners will long be content to be 'hewers of wood and drawers of water': their ambitions are rising, and the immigrant father who is an unskilled worker wants more for his sons. The close association between social class and ethnicity has, therefore, perilous overtones. Should it persist—if Europeans completely monopolize the major prestige positions—then the dangers of communal antagonism will undoubtedly grow.

5

ISRAEL TOMORROW: IMMIGRANTS, ETHNICS, ISRAELIS

THERE are, to be sure, great hazards in predicting a future course of social development. Israel's social or economic progress has, in the past, often confounded the experts: critics have been proved wrong in regard to such issues as continued economic growth, or the vitality of radical institutions such as the *kibbutz*. There is a certain happy optimism, a resiliency, about the Israeli community, and in the past it has proved able to leap over, or bypass, what appeared to be forbidding obstacles. Gloom or doom (if that be the course of prophecy) do not seem appropriate to the Israeli past, where, without question, a great deal has been accomplished.

Prediction is also made difficult by the likely entry of totally new conditions: assessing the present is difficult enough, but to suppose that present-day conditions will continue in the future is likely to be an erroneous assumption. For example, what if peace treaties are signed between Israel and the surrounding Arab states: how would peace affect inter-group relations? What if Russian Jews are permitted to emigrate to Israel? Or how would an economic decline in the West—an American economic depression—alter the course of Israel's social development? Major events such as these may occur in the future, and they would certainly alter the society's emerging character.

In examining some possible future paths, the assumption is necessarily made that social and economic conditions will not change drastically. Three different types of possible future societal organization will be considered: social assimilation,

Levantinization and ethnic pluralism. These three are the alternatives commonly referred to in discussions of Israel's social future, and in this chapter the meanings of these terms, as well as their chances of fulfilment, will be explored. However, before turning to these questions it is first necessary to return to several of the issues raised earlier in this book.

Arabs and Jews, Again

The dominant themes thus far have been veteran-immigrant, and European-Middle Eastern, relations. These are basic social cleavages—but there are others, too, and they merit consideration, however brief. This is particularly the case in regard to Arab-Jewish relations. In the first chapter mention was made of a physical separation between these groups, but questions of Arab-Jewish relations were deferred until now.

Just as the creation of Israel has led to an array of social changes within the Jewish population, so too has it produced widespread changes among Israeli Arabs. For example, population shifts have taken place among Arabs who did not flee the country in 1948; in some cases villagers have moved from their own communities and joined others, so that just as among Jews, some Arab villages are divided between 'veterans' and 'newcomers'. There has also been a movement to the towns and cities, particularly on the part of youngsters who either are attracted by the allure of city life or are unable to find satisfactory employment in their villages.

Village life has itself changed dramatically. An entire array of technological innovations has been introduced: villagers now commonly plough their fields with tractors, and use modern methods of irrigation and seed-selection; rural electrification extends to most Arab villages, and new sources of water have also been tapped. In some communities marketing co-operatives were organized, and small-scale industries have lately been introduced. These innovations, sponsored mainly by the government, or by groups such as the Histadruth, have usually met with a positive reception: villagers are, as a rule, eager to modernize their agricultural techniques. Partly as a result of greater efficiency in farming, and due also to the availability of seasonal and other employment, many Arab

69

villagers have enjoyed a relative economic prosperity during the past decade. Village incomes have grown substantially: the villagers benefit from the general growth in the Israeli economy.

Changes in technology or occupation have also influenced the traditional patterns of village social and political relationships: Arab extended-families have weakened considerably, and there is growing emphasis on individual family units. Conflicts between generations are also typical, as the youngsters actively contest for control of the village. These changes had already begun in the pre-state period, but there can be little doubt that they have intensified in the past decade.

Primary schools in Arab areas now include most children. In villages or towns the children follow a curriculum similar to that of Jewish schoolchildren: Hebrew is taught, and children also learn about the state and its organization. They may also attend high-school, and some have gone on to receive advanced degrees from the Hebrew University and Haifa Technicon. In this sense the educational patterns of Jews and Arabs are similar, although a much smaller proportion of Arabs receive advanced training. However, an Arab youth equipped with higher educational skills is faced with special problems: will Jewish firms, either public or private, employ him? What career channels are open to a minority which is politically suspect?

This problem of the 'Arab intelligentsia' is representative of the dilemma of Arab-Jewish relations: can Israeli Arabs be considered as just another social group, part of the country's general social diversity, or are they rather a dangerous, politically disloyal enclave? Israeli Arabs vote in elections, and their representatives are members of parliament: yet can Arabs be expected to become loyal Israeli citizens, or is it more likely that they are and will remain an alien 'fifth column', awaiting the next opportunity to join in Israel's destruction? It is not easy to give fully satisfactory answers to these questions; one deals mainly with impressions, since these issues have not been studied carefully enough. However, the dominant impression is that the sympathies of Israeli Arabs are overwhelmingly with their fellow-Arabs, and that Arab allegiance is not to the Jewish majority that now rules, but rather with their kinsmen in Egypt or Jordan who promise to liberate them. There may be many exceptions to this impression, but it certainly includes the majority of Arabs.*

These feelings are probably bound to be ascendant. It is too much to expect that a defeated minority will quickly pledge allegiance to those who defeated them, particularly when their brethren in the surrounding countries continue to promise their liberation. The memories of defeat have not subsided, nor have most Arabs made peace with their present lot. Moreover, Israeli government policy has also operated on the assumption that Arabs could not be trusted, that they could not be expected to be loyal to the state. The army has been entrusted with maintaining security in zones of Arab concentration; until recently Arabs were required to obtain a special pass before they could travel from place to place; and the government and allied groups have been reluctant to employ Arabs in positions of trust, in the fear that they were, or would become, spies serving foreign masters. Government policy has inevitably become a kind of 'self-fulfilling prophecy': developing policies on the assumption that Arabs are disloyal excludes them from any roles in which they might display or develop loyalty, and therefore only isolates them even further. It is debatable whether any other policy could in fact bind them closer to the Jewish majority: their estrangement may be so deep, the wounds so bitter, that any policy of integration may be bound to fail. For all of these reasons, it is unlikely that Arab loyalties to Israel have grown deeper in the past decade and a half.

On the level of personal relations, individual Jews and Arabs may come to know one another intimately. There are efforts to develop greater communication between groups—to bridge the gulf between them. On the whole, however, the two groups are rigidly separated from one another and do not develop close personal ties. Arab-Jewish relations are usually formal and hierarchical: Jews usually appear as foremen,

---

* The *Druze*, a small sectarian Arab group, have adapted differently, and seem generally to have adjusted to the new socio-political conditions. Thus, for example, *Druze* units are organized in the army (other Arabs do not serve), and the *Druze* have been freed from other restrictions.

police or judges, and Arabs as unskilled help, or plaintiffs. There are few informal occasions in which Arabs and Jews mix together. For example, marriage between members of the two groups is, in effect, prohibited: authority over marriage is vested in religious officials (there is no civil marriage in Israel) and a rabbi will not perform the marriage ceremony between Arab and Jew. To put it more generally, it is possible that a child growing up in Tel Aviv may never meet an Israeli Arab, and rarely even see an Arab save for an occasional trip to Nazareth or Beersheba. Born of the hatred of war and conquest, members of the two groups generally maintain only peripheral, secondary contacts: each lives in a closed universe, and each distrusts and probably dislikes the other.

This tragic situation will, unfortunately, probably last for as long as a state of war persists between Israel and her neighbours. If normal relations existed between Israel and the Arab states, then Israeli Arabs could be expected to become more fully integrated into Israeli society. It is unlikely that anything can take the place of peace: neither economic prosperity nor the loosening of regulations are likely to have much effect upon Arab loyalty to Israel. When will peace finally come: in ten years, fifty years, never? It is impossible to know. Without peace, however, relations between these groups are likely to be dominated by suspicion and fear.

Controversy Over Religion

Yet another focus of group allegiance, and inter-group tension is formed by the religious and secular elements in the Jewish population. This is an old division, reaching back into the colonization period: in those days, just as now, the Jewish community included a secular majority, and an orthodox religious minority. Mass immigration has maintained this balance: although many Middle Eastern immigrants consider themselves to be 'religious persons', they have not joined the religious parties in overwhelming numbers. Approximately one-sixth of the total votes cast in national elections have been for the candidates of religious parties. This is only a rough index to the extent of religious sentiment, however, since many who are religious may vote for other candidates. The proportions vary from place to place, but perhaps a fifth or even a quarter of the Jewish population might be classed as 'religious'.

Israel's religious problem centres around a continuing controversy regarding the extent to which public life should be ruled by the dicta of orthodox tradition. The religious groups wish to expand the scope of theocratic control—secular groups hope to limit or entirely do away with state religious restrictions —and the results are continued compromises. The extent of religious control has neither expanded nor narrowed appreciably since 1948; rather, an informal kind of status quo has been agreed upon. The understandings reached in the first years following the state's formation continue to be carried out: public transport does not operate on the Sabbath; marriage, divorce and burial are controlled by religious authorities, girls may be conscripted into the army (unless they certify that they are 'religious' and are then exempted), dietary regulations must be followed in state-supported institutions, and so forth. These arrangements have by now become nearly traditional: they are expected and followed, even if they inconvenience many and are bitterly disputed by some. Indeed, the informal agreements are clung to tenaciously. For example, buses may not run on the Sabbath but private taxis do operate: the agreement is that the taxis will pick up passengers only on certain designated streets— and if attempts are made to 'add another street' they may result in rioting.

Why do the majority, who are not orthodox, permit the imposition of restrictions? The usual answer is that the parties in power—socialist, secular groups—have wished to avoid a *kulturkampf*. Differences over religious policies are potentially explosive, and why emphasize yet another issue when the society is already criss-crossed by divisions? Moreover, the socialist parties have found the religious groups to be congenial political partners: it has often been easier to compromise with them than with other parties on the more extreme left or right. In addition, the Jewish populace has mixed feelings regarding 'religion': the majority may be secular, but still it wishes for 'something Jewish' to be preserved in the state. What is distinctively Jewish about Israel: the army, the tax structure, a penchant for archaeology? Shouldn't the Jewish State have 'something' observably Jewish? What will the younger generation know regarding its heritage if Israel turns entirely secular? These questions trouble members of the secular majority, and they have thus far been unwilling to press their numerical advantage. For these reasons a truce exists; there are tacit agreements, and neither side presses new claims too energetically.

The Assimilation Model

There are still other group relations that might usefully be explored: relations between the different segments of the Middle Eastern Jewish groups, or between Christian and Moslem Arabs. Not all topics can be treated in a short essay, however, and it is best to return to the questions posed at the beginning of this chapter: what social and cultural characteristics are likely to become dominant in a future Israeli society? More specifically, what is the likelihood that total social assimilation will take place?

'Total assimilation' has been the goal of the veteran Europeans: this doctrine is represented by the belief that immigrants would give up their previous habits and adopt the traditions of the veteran community. This view is, as was pointed out earlier, the real meaning of the phrase, 'ingathering of exiles'. Born of an optimistic view of man as 'reformable', as well as the fear that veterans would be overwhelmed by the immigrant masses, these expectations have often formed the basis of government social policy.

In order to assess the extent of assimilation, it is first necessary to specify, 'which veterans' and 'which immigrants'. The veterans—it will be recalled—are split between a pioneering and a middle-class sector. It is possible for immigrants to be assimilated within either of these two sectors. As was noted earlier, however, the majority have not followed the pioneering model, but seek instead to fulfil their ambitions within a middle-class style-of-living. In many respects this is an easier mode of accommodation: to become a 'pioneer' requires the adoption of more rigid, demanding new habits, than does a continuation of an immigrant's earlier merchant or craft skills. Although most opt for this model, the speed at which immigrants merge with veterans is extremely variable. These

74

variations are an expression of many factors: there are differences in assimilation between immigrants who cluster together and those who do not, between the 'disaffected' and the 'committed', or between those who marry one another and those who marry members of different immigrant groups.

In general, however, the rate of assimilation is probably more rapid for European immigrants than it is for Middle Easterners: the higher mobility rates of Europeans (as reflected in income and education) draws them more quickly into the expanding middle class, where they meet and soon resemble the veteran Europeans. Differential access to high political position may, in the future, still separate veterans from immigrant Europeans: by means of family ties and other informal links the veterans (and their children) may continue to monopolize key positions in the government-Histadruth-Labour Party axis. But in other spheres of life the veteran and immigrant Europeans grow closer together.

Not so for Middle Easterners, they will probably retain distinctive patterns of behaviour for longer periods of time. So long as they are less mobile socially, they are also less likely to adopt new traditions. And even as they move into middle-class positions, the differences in life-style between, say, Middle Eastern merchants and European merchants, or administrators drawn from the different groups, will also distinguish them. Middle Easterners and Europeans—more specifically, Yemenites, Kurds, Moroccans, Germans, Poles, and so forth—are thus likely to remain part of the Israeli social landscape in the foreseeable future.

There is evidence that this view has recently gained support within the veteran European community itself: there is an increasing awareness that cultural differences do not quickly fade away. Reflecting upon these issues, the Israeli Prime Minister, Levi Eshkol, commented that 'in the past I believed that we would, within ten or fifteen years, succeed in changing the face of Israeli society after we had processed the younger generation through the educational melting-pot—the kindergarten, elementary schools and the post-elementary classes. Now I have come to see this as a long process and a matter of generations.'[1] The encounter with Middle Eastern immigrants may have led to a more mature, less mechanistic, view of cultural difference and change.

A Second View: Levantinization

A very different forecast is sometimes made by Europeans who, it would appear, are uncertain or fearful about the future. This prediction, which is strongly slanted to European values, has sometimes been echoed by persons in high government positions and, although it is not likely to be fulfilled, since it is often voiced it merits consideration.

This forecast, which is referred to as 'Levantinization', promises the exact opposite from assimilation. Levantinization suggests that, in the future, the numerical superiority of Middle Easterners will result in the dominance of a rootless, amoral spirit. The ever-growing Middle Eastern majority (according to this view) adopts only a thin veneer of Western custom, while beneath that veneer there remains the cynical, volatile spirit of the Levant. The ascendance of this Levantine type will finally signal the end of great social dreams: the wish to create the 'good society' will sink under the sheer weight of Middle Eastern numbers. And indeed, so this viewpoint concludes, the cynicism and signs of moral decay already present in Israeli life attest to the growing influence of this Levantine spirit.

The possibility of a 'Levantine future' is very slight. The overwhelming direction of culture is to the West, not the East, and Middle Easterners adopt many of the habits and aspirations of their European brethren. There is no basis for concluding that these changes are merely 'skin deep': when placed in positions of trust, Middle Easterners perform with competence and skill. Nor are there grounds for questioning their sincerity or morality: like Europeans, Middle Easterners also express social ideals and public sensibilities. It is true that these newcomers have not enthusiastically responded to the repeated calls for a renewal of pioneering, or to other slogans of the 1920s and 1930s that are often voiced. But then, most Europeans have themselves turned deaf ears to these pronouncements, and are openly cynical regarding slogans of 'national service' or the 'worker led society'. That these ideologies do not excite Middle Eastern newcomers does not mean that they are insensitive to social progress, but may rather reflect the fact that the slogans themselves are increasingly irrelevant to contemporary life. Besides, it is mainly these immigrants who have fulfilled the old dreams. Middle Easterners predominate in the classic zones of pioneering: more than any other segment of the population they personally experience and achieve the pioneering goals. Certainly this cannot be interpreted as undermining public morality.

Middle Easterners have not injected an amoral or immoral spirit into Israeli life. If, for example, corruption exists in public offices—and to a certain extent there is corruption—the failings are mainly those of Europeans, and not Middle Easterners. The scandals that regularly rock Israeli society mainly involve members of the veteran European élite, not Middle Eastern immigrants. If personal relations are often petty and nasty, or if the bureaucracies are clumsy and irritating, it is not due to the influence of the Middle Eastern newcomers but rather represents the shortcomings of the veteran Europeans. The fearsome spectre of 'Levantinization' seems little more than a rationalization of the inner crisis facing the dominant European group. Life in Israel is changing, and some of the old dreams may not become realized: Middle Easterners therefore become a convenient scapegoat, a supposedly alien group upon which one may focus blame.

For all these reasons Levantinization seems an unlikely future course for Israeli society. Israel has certainly become different since hundreds of thousands of Middle Easterners migrated there; these 'masses' are making and will continue to make a deep impression upon the country's character. Yet the Middle Eastern majority moves in the direction of the West, and if the quality of life about them is substantial they may be expected to make a significant contribution to it.

The Pluralistic Future

The third course, a type of plural society, seems more probable. According to this view, ethnic-group associations and ethnic identity are not likely to disappear in the future, but rather will continue to have meaning for immigrants and their descendants. The European veterans will retain their pre-eminent positions, but, in addition, other culturally defined groups will retain a distinctive sense of difference. Israel will not lose its ties with Western culture; on the contrary, as networks of universal communication expand, the present-day roots in Western civilization may grow even deeper. The major public institutions—government on a local and national level, the economic system, the schools, arts and sciences—will continue to be expressed in a Western idiom. For non-Europeans, the direction of change will also continue to be towards the West: the lifestyles of all groups will be modelled after a Western pattern. Yet even as this process of cultural universalism takes place, the separate traditions of immigrant groups will continue to hold meaning for the immigrants and their children.

Cultural persistence derives from a variety of factors. In the first place, immigrants who are ambivalent, disaffected or apathetic do not enthusiastically embrace the veteran traditions: these states of mind do not weld the immigrants closer to the veteran groups. Such responses will persist for so long as the conditions that give rise to them are present in the society. If, therefore, a sense of discrimination or exclusion extends to second, third or succeeding generations, then apathy and disaffection may also be expected to persist. Moreover, and of equal importance, the prevailing ethnic residence clusters, the prevailing marriage choices, as well as the stratification in income and residence also forecasts the continued presence of distinguishable ethnic groups. While Yemenites marry other Yemenites, or Kurds concentrate in particular neighbourhoods, the links between members of each of these groups are likely to remain significant. Differentials in income, education and political mobility also suggest that not all youngsters become *sabras*: if European youngsters go on to attend university, while Moroccans become apprentice mechanics, then both groups will retain their present sense of separation. The *sabra* model may become increasingly influential, but for as long as contemporary economic and political conditions persist the model will not encompass all youngsters. Finally, group differences will continue to be expressed since some cultural traditions are prized and therefore preserved: immigrants from both Germany and Tunisia, for example, find worth and meaning in their own cultural heritage, and they continue to transmit those traditions to their children. For all of these reasons the likelihood is that, in the near future at least, Israel will continue to be a multi-ethnic, or plural, society.

Such a society will not, of course, merely be a duplication of other multi-ethnic societies. The size of the country and its population, the common Jewish bonds that draw persons together, the important role of ideology, ties with overseas Jewish communities, uneasy relations with her neighbours: all these conditions lend Israel a special, distinctive character. As in other plural societies, individuals will have a variety of allegiances, and the meaning of 'being Yemenite' or 'being Hungarian' will no doubt become altered in the future. Yet—and this is the major point—ethnicity is likely to persist in the foreseeable future.

This may be the future form of Israeli society: but what of the quality of life expressed within it? The early European colonists dreamed of a new kind of society; they held the vision of a vital, rejuvenated mankind. Will a multi-ethnic Israel be able to achieve those dreams, or any other dreams? Will it be able to draw on the richness in cultural differences, and create new forms of social relationships—or will it sink into petty squabbling, or a dull nationalism, or an equally dull nostalgia over the 'good old days' of pioneering drama? There can be no authoritative answers to these questions: to comment upon them is merely to speculate, and the speculation may be grossly in error. None the less, if one is to judge from the past, Israeli society has been vital and creative: the *kibbutz*, the Histadruth, perhaps even the army, have all been creative social institutions. These particular forms were, however, born of conditions different from the contemporary scene: Israel is now a 'post-pioneering' society, and the dramatic experience of national rebirth belongs largely to the past. The issues of daily life appear more mundane and uninspiring in comparison: increasing participation in public affairs, or developing a superior administrative system, pale in contrast with 'conquering the desert' or making a 'new type of man'. Yet these issues, and others like them, are now relevant, and they cry out for inventive solutions. Indeed, they demand a new type of idealism; namely, the courage to re-think traditional answers, and to develop different, genuinely radical approaches to the problems of daily living. To judge from past experience, one may be hopeful that new paths will be found. There is always the chance that today's niggling issues—and they *are* often niggling and depressing—will yet be transcended. The novelist Dan Jacobson expressed this well in a recent essay: he finds that there is 'a constant and unending struggle . . . to keep up standards . . . The Israelis have not forgotten that there are standards, and are trying fitfully, erratically, wrongheadedly often, but always determinedly, to find out what the standards are.'[1] With this moral concern, a multi-ethnic Israel may well discover imaginative ways to resolve the issues that she, and indeed so many other nations, now face.

References

1: Introduction

[1] Radio-broadcast transcript, 'A Conversation in Sderot: The Two Cultures' (in Hebrew), *Ammot*, Vol. III, December, 1963, p. 7.
[2] Ibid., p. 7.

2: Cultural Foundations

[1] Isaiah Berlin, 'The Origins of Israel', *The Middle East in Transition*, edited by Walter Z. Lacquer, London, Routledge and Kegan Paul, 1948, pp. 208–13.
[2] Ibid., p. 210.
[3] *Statistical Abstract of Israel, 1963*, Jerusalem, The Central Bureau of Statistics, 1963, pp. 15, 18.
[4] Ibid., p. 45.
[5] Ibid., p. 44.
[6] The estimate of 740,000 Arabs is given in Dan Patinken's *The Israel Economy: The First Decade*, Jerusalem, The Jerusalem Post Press, 1960, and is based upon figures collected by Avner Hovne.
[7] *Statistical Abstract of Israel*, 1963, p. 25.
[8] Ibid., pp. 408–9.
[9] Dan Patinken, *The Israel Economy: The First Decade*, p. 38.
[10] Ibid., p. 41.

3: Immigrant Responses

[1] See Walter Zenner, 'Ambivalence and Self-Image Among Oriental Jews in Israel', *Jewish Journal of Sociology*, Vol. V, No. 2, pp. 214–23.
[2] *Statistical Abstract of Israel*, 1961, Jerusalem, The Central Bureau of Statistics, 1961, p. 93.
[3] Ibid., p. 365.
[4] A. Doron, 'Poverty in Israel' (in Hebrew), *Ammot*, Vol. II, No. 4, February–March, 1964, p. 9.

[5] A. Katz and A. Zloczower, 'Ethnic Continuity in an Israeli Town', *Human Relations*, Vol. XIV, No. 4, 1961, p. 296.

[6] J. Shaval, 'Patterns of Inter-group Tension Affinity', *International Social Science Bulletin*, Vol. VIII, No. 1, 1956, pp. 75-126.

[7] S. N. Eisenstadt, *The Absorption of Immigrants*, Glencoe, The Free Press, 1955, p. 148.

[8] Ibid., p. 155.

[9] Ibid., pp. 145-7.

[10] N. Rejwan, 'Israel's Communal Controversy—an Oriental's Appraisal', *Midstream*, Vol. X, No. 2, June 1964, p. 26.

4: Patterns of Mobility

[1] G. Hanoch, 'Income Differentials in Israel', *Fifth Report 1959 and 1960, The Falk Project for Economic Research in Israel*, Jerusalem, 1961, pp. 37-125.

[2] Ibid., p. 46.

[3] Ibid., pp. 117-18.

[4] Ibid., p. 69.

[5] Ibid., p. 68.

[6] Ibid., p. 58.

[7] *Statistical Abstract of Israel, 1963*, Jerusalem: The Central Bureau of Statistics, 1963, p. 79.

5: Israel Tomorrow: Immigrants, Ethnics, Israelis

[1] D. Jacobson, 'Zion Revisited', *Commentary*, Vol. XXVIII, 1959, p. 3.